Vehicles

Experiments in Synthetic Psychology

Valentino Braitenberg

The MIT Press
Cambridge, Massachusetts
London, England

Technical drawings by Ladina Ribi and Claudia
Martin-Schubert.

This book was set in Linotron 202 Sabon by Achorn
Graphic Services and printed and bound by Halliday
Lithograph in the United States of America

Library of Congress Cataloging in Publication Data
Braitenberg, Valentino.
    Vehicles, experiments in synthetic psychology.

    "Bradford books"—Series t.p.
    Bibliography: p.
    1. Neurophysiology. 2. Psychology, Physiological.
1. Title. [DNLM: 1. Psychophysiology. WL 103 B8148V]
QP356.B74 1984 152 84-9727
ISBN 0-262-02208-7

Date Due

ILL 4-3-91			
MAY - 3 2000			

Vehicles

⊔⌐ Bradford Books

Edward C. T. Walker, Editor. Explorations in THE BIOLOGY OF LANGUAGE. 1979.

Daniel C. Dennett. BRAINSTORMS. 1979.

Charles E. Marks. COMMISSUROTOMY, CONSCIOUSNESS AND UNITY OF MIND. 1980.

John Haugeland, Editor. MIND DESIGN. 1981.

Ned Block, Editor. IMAGERY. 1981.

Roger N. Shepard and Lynn A. Cooper. MENTAL IMAGES AND THEIR TRANSFORMATIONS. 1982.

Irvin Rock. THE LOGIC OF PERCEPTION. 1983.

Elliot Sober, Editor. CONCEPTUAL ISSUES IN EVOLUTIONARY BIOLOGY. 1984.

Paul M. Churchland. MATTER AND CONSCIOUSNESS. 1984.

Owen D. Flanagan. THE SCIENCE OF MIND. 1984.

Zenon W. Pylyshyn. COMPUTATION AND COGNITION. 1984.

Robert N. Brandon and Richard M. Burian, Editors. GENES, ORGANISMS, POPULATIONS. 1984.

Ruth Garrett Millikan. LANGUAGE, THOUGHT AND OTHER BIOLOGICAL CATEGORIES. 1984.

Daniel C. Dennett. ELBOW ROOM: FREE WILL WORTH WANTING. 1984.

Valentino Braitenberg. VEHICLES: EXPERIMENTS IN SYNTHETIC PSYCHOLOGY. 1984.

Elliot Sober. THE NATURE OF SELECTION. 1984.

Alle mie creature

Contents

Foreword

Valentino Braitenberg is a cybernetician, a neuroanatomist, and a musician. He seeks to understand how the beautiful structures of the brain constitute a machine that can enable us to exhibit such skilled behavior as that involved in playing music. Since the early 1960s, I have turned to Valentino for detailed neuroanatomy and for lively essays that cut away the technical details to illuminate the key issues of what we may call cybernetics or artificial intelligence or cognitive science.

One of the most exciting of these essays had the most formidable of titles: "Taxis, Kinesis and Decussation," published in 1965. *Taxis* is the reflex-oriented movement of a freely moving organism in relation to a source of stimulation; *kinesis*, by contrast, is movement that lacks orientation but depends on the intensity of stimulation; and a *decussation* is a band of nerve fibers that connects one half of the body to the opposite half of the brain. The title was forbidding, the essay was delightful. By designing little vehicles that moved around in response to smell and vision, Braitenberg gave his readers vivid insights into how the brain might have evolved so that olfactory input goes to the same side of the brain while vision, touch, and hearing send their input to the opposite side of the brain.

Having shared this paper with friends and students over the years, I was delighted to hear from Valentino, at a workshop in 1983, that it had provided the nucleus for this book. *Vehicles: Experiments in Synthetic Psychology* is fun to read, and this fun is heightened by the incredible illustrations of Maciek Albrecht. But it is serious fun and will help many people, specialist and layman alike, gain broad insights into the ways in which intelligence evolved to guide interaction with a complex world.

Michael A. Arbib
Amherst, Massachusetts

Vehicles

Introduction

Let the Problem of the Mind Dissolve in Your Mind

This is an exercise in fictional science, or science fiction, if you like that better. Not for amusement: science fiction in the service of science. Or just science, if you agree that fiction is part of it, always was, and always will be as long as our brains are only minuscule fragments of the universe, much too small to hold all the facts of the world but not too idle to speculate about them.

I have been dealing for many years with certain structures within animal brains that seemed to be interpretable as pieces of computing machinery because of their simplicity and/or regularity. Much of this work is only interesting if you are yourself involved in it. At times, though, in the back of my mind, while I was counting fibers in the visual ganglia of the fly or synapses in the cerebral cortex of the mouse, I felt knots untie, distinctions dissolve, difficulties disappear, difficulties I had experienced much earlier when I still held my first naive philosophical approach to the problem of the mind. This process of purification has been, over the years, a delightful experience. The text I want you to read is designed to convey some of this to you, if you are prepared to follow me not through a world of real brains but through a toy world that we will create together.

We will talk only about machines with very simple internal structures, too simple in fact to be interesting from the point of view of mechanical or electrical engineering. Interest arises, rather, when we look at these machines or vehicles as if they were animals in a natural environment. We will be tempted, then, to use psychological language in describing their behavior. And yet we know very well that there is nothing in these vehicles that we have not put in ourselves. This will be an interesting educational game.

Our vehicles may move in water by jet propulsion. Or you may prefer to imagine them moving somewhere between galaxies, with negligible gravitational pull. Remember, however, that their jets must expel matter in order to function at all, and this implies replenishment of the food stores within the vehicles, which might be a problem between galaxies. This suggests vehicles moving on the surface of the earth through an agricultural landscape where they have good support and can easily find the food or fuel they need. (Indeed the first few chapters here conjure up images of vehicles swimming around in the water, while later what comes to mind are little carts moving on hard surfaces. This is no accident, if the evolution of vehicles 1 to 14 in any way reflects the evolution of animal species.)

It does not matter. Get used to a way of thinking in which the hardware of the realization of an idea is much less important than the idea itself. Norbert Wiener was emphatic about this when he formulated the title of his famous book: *Cybernetics, or Control and Communication in Animals and Machines.*

Getting Around

Vehicle 1 is equipped with one sensor and one motor (figure 1). The connection is a very simple one. The more there is of the quality to which the sensor is tuned, the faster the motor goes. Let the quality be temperature and let the force exerted by the motor be exactly proportionate to the absolute temperature (the temperature above zero degrees Kelvin) measured by the sensor. The vehicle will move, wherever it is (the absolute temperature is nowhere equal to zero), in the direction in which it happens to be pointing. It will slow down in cold regions and speed up where it is warm.

Here we have introduced a bit of Aristotelian physics. Aristotle, like everybody else between this ancient Greek philosopher and the less ancient Italian physicist Galileo, thought that the speed of a moving body is proportionate to the force that drives it. This is true in most instances, namely when there is friction to slow down the vehicle. Normally friction will see to it that the velocity becomes zero in the absence of any force, that it will stay at a certain small value for a certain small force, at a higher value for a higher force, and so forth.

Of course, as you all know, this is not true for heavenly bodies

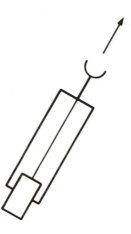

Figure 1

Vehicle 1, the simplest vehicle. The speed of the motor (rectangular box at the tail end) is controlled by a sensor (half circle on a stalk, at the front end). Motion is always forward, in the direction of the arrow, except for perturbations.

(especially if you don't invest astronomical time in observing them). Their velocity is a complicated result of all the forces that ever hit them. This is another reason for letting our vehicles move in water or on the surface of the earth rather than in outer space.

In this Aristotelian world our vehicle number 1 may even come to rest. This will happen when it enters a cold region where the force exerted by its motor, being proportionate to the temperature, becomes smaller than the frictional force.

Once you let friction come into the picture, other amazing things may happen. In outer space Vehicle 1 would move on a straight course with varying speed (the gravitational pull of neighboring galaxies averages out to nothing). Not so on earth. The friction, which is nothing but the sum of all the microscopic forces that arise in a situation too messy to be analyzed in detail, may not be quite symmetrical. As the vehicle pushes forward against frictional forces, it will deviate from its course. In the long run it will be seen to move in a complicated trajectory, curving one way or the other without apparent good reason. If it is very small, its motion will be quite erratic, similar to "Brownian motion," only with a certain drive added.

Imagine, now, what you would think if you saw such a vehicle swimming around in a pond. It is restless, you would say, and does not like warm water. But it is quite stupid, since it is not able to turn back to the nice cold spot it overshot in its restlessness. Anyway, you would say, it is ALIVE, since you have never seen a particle of dead matter move around quite like that.

Vehicle 2

Fear and Aggression

Vehicle 2 is generally similar to Vehicle 1 except that it has two sensors, one on each side, and two motors, right and left (figure 2). You may think of it as being a descendant of Vehicle 1 through some incomplete process of biological reduplication: two of the earlier brand stuck together side by side. Again, the more the sensors are excited, the faster the motors run.

Of course you notice right away that we can make three kinds of such vehicles, depending on whether we connect (a) each sensor to the motor on the same side, (b) each sensor to the motor on the opposite side, or (c) both sensors to both motors. We can immediately dismiss case (c), for this is nothing but a somewhat more luxurious version of Vehicle 1. The difference between (a) and (b), however, is very interesting.

Consider (a) first. This vehicle will spend more time in the places where there is less of the stuff that excites its sensors and will speed up when it is exposed to higher concentrations. If the source of the stuff (say, light in the case of light sensors) is directly ahead, the vehicle may hit the source unless it is deflected from its course. If the source is to one side (figure 3), one of the sensors, the one nearer to the source, is excited more than the other. The corresponding

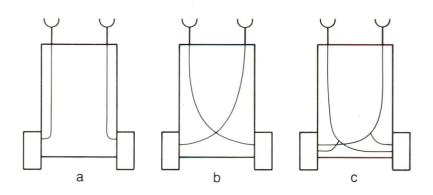

Figure 2
Vehicle 2, with two motors and two sensors; otherwise like Vehicle 1. The connections differ in a, b, and c.

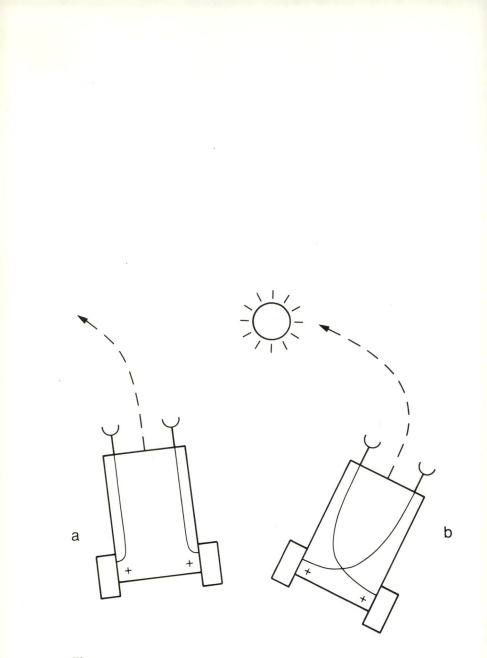

Figure 3
Vehicles 2a and 2b in the vicinity of a source (circle with rays emanating from it). Vehicle 2b orients toward the source, 2a away from it.

motor will work harder. And as a consequence the vehicle will turn away from the source.

Now let us try the other scheme of sensory-motor connections, (b) in figure 3. No change if the source is straight ahead. If it is to one side, however, we notice a difference with respect to Vehicle 2a. Vehicle 2b will turn toward the source and eventually hit it. There is no escaping: as long as 2b stays in the vicinity of the source, no matter how it stumbles and hesitates, it will hit the source frontally in the end. Only in the unlikely case that a strong perturbation in its course makes it turn exactly away from the source, and no further perturbation occurs, can it escape its fate.

Let Vehicles 2a and 2b move around in their world for a while and watch them. Their characters are quite opposite. Both DISLIKE sources. But 2a becomes restless in their vicinity and tends to avoid them, escaping until it safely reaches a place where the influence of the source is scarcely felt. Vehicle 2a is a COWARD, you would say. Not so Vehicle 2b. It, too, is excited by the presence of sources, but resolutely turns toward them and hits them with high velocity, as if it wanted to destroy them. Vehicle 2b is AGGRESSIVE, obviously.

Vehicle 3

Love

The violence of Vehicle 2b, no less than the cowardice of its companion 2a, are traits that call for improvement. There is something very crude about a vehicle that can only be excited by the things it smells (or sees or feels or hears) and knows no soothing or relaxing stimuli. What comes to mind is to introduce some inhibition in the connections between the sensors and the motors, switching the sign of the influence from positive to negative. This will let the motor slow down when the corresponding sensor is activated. Again we can make two variants, one with straight and one with crossed connections (figure 4). Both will slow down in the presence of a strong stimulus and race where the stimulus is weak. They will therefore spend more time in the vicinity of the source than away from it. They will actually come to rest in the immediate vicinity of the source.

But here we notice a difference between the vehicle with straight connections and the one with crossed connections. Approaching the source, the first (figure 4a) will orient toward it, since on an oblique course the sensor nearer to the source will slow down the motor on the same side, producing a turn toward that side. The vehicle with straight connections will come to rest facing the

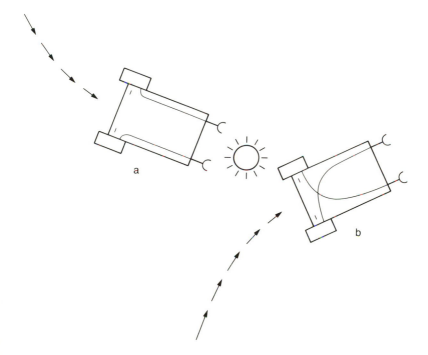

Figure 4
Vehicle 3, with inhibitory influence of the sensors on the motors.

source. The vehicle with crossed connections (figure 4b) for analogous reasons will come to rest facing away from the source and may not stay there very long, since a slight perturbation could cause it to drift away from the source. This would lessen the source's inhibitory influence, causing the vehicle to speed up more and more as it gets away.

You will have no difficulty giving names to this sort of behavior. These vehicles LIKE the source, you will say, but in different ways. Vehicle 3a LOVES it in a permanent way, staying close by in quiet admiration from the time it spots the source to all future time. Vehicle 3b, on the other hand, is an EXPLORER. It likes the nearby source all right, but keeps an eye open for other, perhaps stronger sources, which it will sail to, given a chance, in order to find a more permanent and gratifying appeasement.

But this is not yet the full development of Vehicle 3. We are now ready to make a more complete model using all the behavioral traits at our disposal. Call it Vehicle 3c. We give it not just one pair of sensors but four pairs, tuned to different qualities of the environment, say light, temperature, oxygen concentration, and amount of organic matter (figure 5). Now we connect the first pair to the motors with uncrossed excitatory connections, as in Vehicle 2a, the second pair with crossed excitatory connections, as in Vehicle 2b, and the third and fourth pairs with inhibitory connections, crossed and uncrossed, as in Vehicles 3b and 3a.

This is now a vehicle with really interesting behavior. It dislikes high temperature, turns away from hot places, and at the same time seems to dislike light bulbs with even greater passion, since it turns toward them and destroys them. On the other hand it definitely seems to prefer a well-oxygenated environment and one containing many organic molecules, since it spends much of its time in such places. But it is in the habit of moving elsewhere when the supply of either organic matter or (especially) oxygen is low. You cannot help admitting that Vehicle 3c has a system of VALUES, and, come to

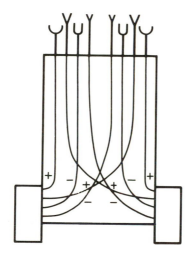

Figure 5
A multisensorial vehicle of brand 3c.

think of it, KNOWLEDGE, since some of the habits it has, like destroying light bulbs, may look quite knowledgeable, as if the vehicle knows that light bulbs tend to heat up the environment and consequently make it uncomfortable to live in. It also looks as if it knows about the possibility of making energy out of oxygen and organic matter because it prefers places where these two commodities are available.

But, you will say, this is ridiculous: knowledge implies a flow of information from the environment into a living being or at least into something like a living being. There was no such transmission of information here. We were just playing with sensors, motors, and connections: the properties that happened to emerge may look like knowledge but really are not. We should be careful with such words.

You are right. We will explain in a later chapter (on Vehicle 6) how knowledge may enter a system of connections. And we will introduce an alternative way of incorporating knowledge into the system in our chapter on Vehicle 7. In any case, once knowledge is incorporated, the resulting vehicle may look and behave quite like our Vehicle 3c.

Meanwhile I invite you to consider the enormous wealth of different properties that we may give Vehicle 3c by choosing various sensors and various combinations of crossed and uncrossed, excitatory and inhibitory, connections.

If you consider the possibility of strong and weak influences from the sensors to the motors, you realize that the variety becomes even greater. The vehicle may not care much about light but care very much about temperature. Its sense of smell may be much keener for organic matter than it is for oxygen or vice versa. And there may be many more than just four pairs of sensors and four sensory qualities: the vehicles may be equipped with all sorts of shrewd detectors of energy and of chemicals. But this is best discussed in connection with a new idea incorporated in the vehicles of the next chapter.

Vehicle 4

Values and Special Tastes

We are now in a position to create a new brand of vehicle, starting from all the varieties of Vehicle 3, by working on the connections between sensors and motors. They were, up to now, of two very simple kinds: the more the sensor was excited, the faster the corresponding motor ran, or, alternatively, the more the sensor was excited, the slower the motor ran. We did not care what the rules of the dependence were, as long as they were of the nature "the more, the more" or "the more, the less." The vast class of mathematical functions describing such dependences is sometimes called monotonic. Obviously, there is something very simple-minded about creatures governed by such unconditioned likes or dislikes, and we can easily see how such the-more-the-merrier behavior could lead to disaster. Think what happens in the case of a tendency to follow downhill slopes!

Let us consider the following improvement. The activation of a certain sensor will make the corresponding motor run faster, but only up to a point, where the speed of the motor reaches a maximum. Beyond this point, if the sensor is activated even more strongly, the speed will decrease again (figure 6). The same sort of dependence, with a maximum efficiency at a certain level of sensor

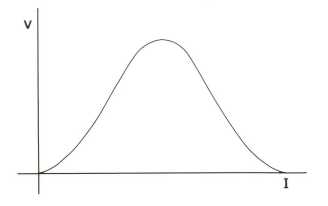

Figure 6
A nonlinear dependence of the speed of the motor V on the intensity of stimulation I, with a maximum for a certain intensity.

activation, can be engineered for the inhibitory connections between sensor and motor. We may set the maximum efficiency of the various sensors at any level we choose, and we may even play with dependences having more than one maximum. Any vehicle constructed according to this prescription we will assign to a new brand, labeled 4a. Of course, if you like, you can keep some of the connections of the old monotonic type and mix them with the nonmonotonic ones in every possible combination.

You will have a hard time imagining the variety of behavior displayed by the vehicles of brand 4a. A 4a vehicle might navigate toward a source (as Vehicle 2b would) and then turn away when the stimulus becomes strong, circle back and then turn away over and over again, perhaps describing a trajectory in the form of a figure eight. Or it might orbit around the source at a fixed distance, like a satellite around the earth, its course being corrected toward the source by a weaker stimulus and away from the source by a stronger stimulus, depending on whether the stimulus intensity is on one side or the other of the maximum describing the sensory-motor dependence (figure 7). Vehicle 4a might like one sort of stimulus when it is weak but not when it is too strong; it might like another stimulus better the stronger it becomes. It might turn away from a weak smell and destroy the source of a strong one. It might visit in alternation a source of smell and a source of sound, turning away from both with a change of temperature.

Watching vehicles of brand 4a in a landscape of sources, you will be delighted by their complicated trajectories. And I am sure you will feel that their motives and tastes are much too varied and intricate to be understood by the observer. These vehicles, you will say, are governed by INSTINCTS of various sorts and, alas, we just don't know how Nature manages to embody instincts into a piece of brain.

You forget, of course, that we have ourselves designed these vehicles.

But instincts are a lowly sort of behavior anyway. We can do better. Let us improve on type 4a by adding a new sort of connection between sensors and motors. This time the influence of the sensor on the motor is no longer smooth; there are definite breaks. There might be a range of intensities of sensory stimulation for which the motor is not activated at all and then, under stronger stimuli, the motors are running at full speed. Or else, there might be smooth changes of motor activation for certain ranges, with abrupt changes in between. A very lifelike pattern would be: no activation up to a threshold value of the stimulus, and increasing activation beyond the threshold, starting with a certain fixed minimum (figure 8). You are by now experienced in the art of creative invention and will have no difficulty dreaming up more schemes of this sort.

In a way these new vehicles, which we call 4b, are already contained in the vast class of vehicles 4a, since abruptness of behavior can of course be simulated with any degree of approximation by functional dependences that are in reality, mathematically speak-

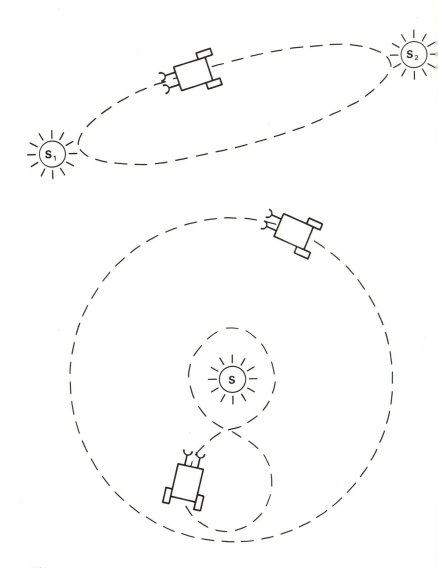

Figure 7
Trajectories of vehicles of brand 4a around or between sources.

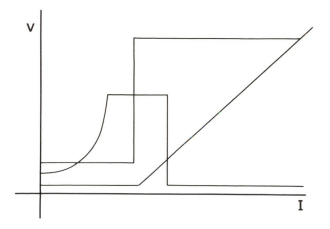

Figure 8
Various bizarre kinds of dependence of the speed of the motor (ordinate) on the intensity of stimulation (abscissa) in Vehicle 4b.

ing, continuous. Moreover, if friction plays a role, as we have already decided it should, thresholds in motor activation would ensue naturally: the vehicle will start moving only when the force exerted by the motor exceeds a certain value, sufficient to overcome the initial friction.

Whatever their origin, thresholds in some behavior patterns make a lot of difference in the eye of the observer. These creatures, the observer would say, ponder over their DECISIONS. When you come close to them with a lure, it takes them some time to get going. Yet once they have decided, they can act quite quickly. They do indeed seem to act in a spontaneous way: none of this passive being attracted one way or the other that was so obvious in the vehicles of the more lowly types. You would almost be tempted to say: where decisions are being made, there must be a WILL to make them. Why not? For all we know, this is not the worst criterion for establishing the existence of free will.

Vehicle 5

Logic

At this point we are ready to make a fundamental discovery. We have gathered evidence for what I would like to call the "law of uphill analysis and downhill invention." What I mean is this. It is pleasurable and easy to create little machines that do certain tricks. It is also quite easy to observe the full repertoire of behavior of these machines—even if it goes beyond what we had originally planned, as it often does. But it is much more difficult to start from the outside and to try to guess internal structure just from the observation of behavior. It is actually impossible in theory to determine exactly what the hidden mechanism is without opening the box, since there are always many different mechanisms with identical behavior. Quite apart from this, analysis is more difficult than invention in the sense in which, generally, induction takes more time to perform than deduction: in induction one has to search for the way, whereas in deduction one follows a straightforward path.

A psychological consequence of this is the following: when we analyze a mechanism, we tend to overestimate its complexity. In the uphill process of analysis, a given degree of complexity offers more resistance to the workings of our mind than it would if we encountered it downhill, in the process of invention. We have already seen this happen when the observer of Vehicle 4b conjectured that the vehicle does some thinking before it reaches a decision, suggesting complicated internal processes where in reality there was nothing but a threshold device waiting for sufficient activation. The patterns of behavior described in the vehicles of type 4a undoubtedly suggest much more complicated machinery than that which was actually used in designing them.

We may now take pleasure in this and create simple "brains" for our vehicles, which will indeed (as experience shows) tax the mind of even the most playful analyst. All we have to do is introduce special elements, called threshold devices, which will be either interposed between sensors and motors or connected to each other in complexes that receive some input from the sensors and give some output to the motors.

The individual threshold device is of the simplest sort: it gives no output if its input line carries a signal below the threshold, and it gives full output beyond the threshold. We will also use another variety giving output all the time unless the input carries a signal above the threshold. Each of these devices is fitted with a knob which may be turned to set the threshold, so that the input would become effective with one, two, or any specified number of input activation units. (The word threshold of course implies that, for a given threshold value, any input stronger than the one specified would also be effective.)

We are not limited to the types of connections through which the threshold devices activate each other. We can also use another kind, call them "inhibitory," which counteract the activation that comes from other sources (figure 9).

In order to make a brain out of threshold devices, we may connect them together one to one, or many to one, or one to many, or many to one and one to many, in whichever way we like. When you are designing brains, it is important for you to know that in one of

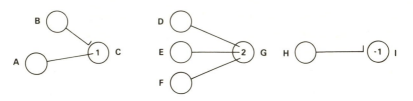

Figure 9

How threshold devices act on each other. Explanation of symbols: The circles stand for threshold devices. The L-shaped fiber between B and C stands for inhibition; the penetrating fiber from A to C means activation. Each active element contributes one unit of activation to the element (threshold device) to which it sends an activating connection. The threshold device becomes active when the activation reaches at least the threshold value indicated within the circle. An inhibitory connection from an active element subtracts 1 from the sum of all the units of activation reaching the same target element. A negative threshold (or threshold 0) implies activity in the absence of external activation. Such an element can be silenced by a corresponding amount of inhibition.

these threshold devices the output does not appear immediately upon activation of the input, but only after a short delay, say one tenth of a second. During this time the gadget performs its little calculation, which consists of comparing the quantity of its activation with its threshold.

You can already guess some of the things that a vehicle fitted with this sort of brain can do, but you will still be surprised when you see it in action. The vehicle may sit there for hours and then suddenly stir when it sights an olive green vehicle that buzzes at a certain frequency and never moves faster than 5cm/sec. Since our brand 5 vehicle is not interested in any other vehicles, you might say that the olive green vehicle is its special friend. You will have to conclude that Vehicle 5 has something like proper nouns in his mind, NAMES that refer to very particular objects, like James, Calcutta, or Jupiter.

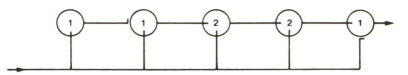

Figure 10a

A network that gives a signal when a burst of 3 pulses presents itself, preceded and followed by a pause.

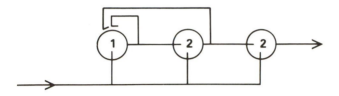

Figure 10b

A network of threshold devices that emits a pulse for every third pulse in a row in the input.

But Vehicle 5 can do much more than that. It can count (figure 10). It may associate only with groups of four vehicles, not more and not less, to make a party of five. Or it may visit every tenth source it encounters on its way. Or it may turn away from a vehicle whose number of sensors is a multiple of seven, implying that such vehicles bring bad luck. In some way, it seems to operate with NUMBERS.

If you fit such a vehicle with a very large number of shrewdly connected threshold devices, you may get it to play a passable game of chess. Or you may make it solve puzzles in LOGIC or prove theorems in euclidean geometry. You realize what I am driving at: with enough threshold devices it can do anything a computer can do, and computers can be made to do almost everything.

But where is the memory, some of you will ask, realizing that most of the activities of a digital computer consist of putting data into memory, taking the data out again to perform some calculation, putting the results back into the memory, and so forth. The answer: there is room for memory in a network of threshold devices, if it is large enough. Imagine a threshold device connected to a sensor for red light. When it is activated by the red light, it activates another threshold device which in turn is connected back to the first device. Once a red light is sighted, the two devices will activate one another forever. Take a wire from the output of one of the two threshold devices and connect it to a bell: the ringing of the bell then signals the fact that at some time in the past this particular vehicle sailed in the vicinity of a source of red light.

This is an elementary sort of MEMORY. It is not difficult to understand how out of such elementary memory stores (consisting of reciprocally connected threshold devices) complex memories can be synthesized, with the possibility of storing extremely complex events. But there is a limit to the quantity of facts the vehicle can store this way. For instance, when storing numbers, if the vehicle has a bank of ten elementary memory devices, it cannot fit any number that has more than ten digits (in binary notation), since each elementary device can at most remember one digit by being active or inactive ("one bit of information").

There is a trick that can be used by our brand 5 vehicles to overcome the intrinsic limitation of their storage capacity. Imagine a vehicle involved in a calculation in which numbers occur that are much larger than the number of parts in the vehicle's own interior. You might think that such a task would be forever beyond the comprehension of that particular vehicle. Not so if we employ the following strategy. Let's transfer our vehicle to a large, sandy beach. The vehicle can crawl on the beach, leaving marks in the sand indicating the succession of digits in the large numbers that emerge from its calculations. Then it can crawl back, following its own track, to read off the digits and put them back into the calculation.

The vehicle is never able to comprehend these large numbers at any one moment. But using itself as an instrument in a larger scheme involving the environment, and partly directed by it, it ends up with the correct result. (Of course, to be on the safe side, we must suppose that the sandy surface has no limits.) If you want a concrete example, think of the vehicle calculating the difference (small enough for it to comprehend) between two large numbers, which it can produce but not comprehend. It will produce one number by leaving marks on its way along the beach. It will produce the other number on its way back. And then it will measure the difference by counting the number of marks that are in default or in excess of the first number.

Later on, we will learn how to incorporate into a vehicle something quite analogous to the sand outside, and almost as boundless in its capacity.

Selection, the Impersonal Engineer

In this chapter things get slightly out of hand. You may regret this, but you will soon notice that it is a good idea to give chance a chance in the further creation of new brands of vehicles. This will make available a source of intelligence that is much more powerful than any engineering mind.

Out of the collection of vehicles that we have produced for the purposes of our experimentation, we will choose some of the more complicated specimens and put them onto a large table. Of course there will also be some sources of light, sound, smell, and so forth on the table, some of them fixed and some of them moving. And there will be various shapes or landmarks, including the cliff that signals the end of the table top.

Now you and I will gather a plentiful supply of materials (tin, plastic, threshold devices, wheels, motors, sensors, wires, screws and bolts) and proceed to build vehicles, taking as our models vehicles that we pick from the ones circulating on the table. Each time we copy a vehicle, we will put both the model and its copy back on the table, pick up another vehicle, copy it, and so on. Of course we will not pick up vehicles that have fallen on the floor because they have proved their own inability to cope with the environment. We will be careful to produce vehicles at a pace that roughly matches the rate at which vehicles fall off the table, to prevent the race from dying out, on one hand, and to prevent the table from becoming unduly crowded, on the other.

Note that while we are playing this game, we won't have time to test the behavior or to study the wiring, let alone to understand the logic of the vehicles that we pick up as models for copying. Nor should we. All we are asked to do is to slavishly connect the parts according to the pattern in the model.

Note also that when we do this in a hurry, we are bound to make occasional mistakes. It may be our fault when our copy of a perfectly well-tested vehicle falls off the table as soon as we put it down. But it is also possible that we will unwittingly introduce a particularly shrewd variation into the pattern of connections, so that our copy will survive forever while the original may turn out to be unfit for survival after all.

It does seem surprising that errors arising in the sloppy execution of a task should act as germs for improvement. What is less astonishing is the creative power of a special sort of error consisting of new combinations of partial mechanisms, each of which is not disrupted in its own well-tested structure. This can easily happen when we pick up one vehicle as a model for one part of the brain and then by mistake pick up another vehicle as a model for another part of the brain. Such errors have a much greater chance of transcending the intelligence of the original plan.

This is an important point. If the lucky accidents live on forever, they will also have a multitude of descendants, for they will stay on the table all the time while the less lucky ones come and go. Therefore, they have a much greater chance of being picked up by the copyists as models for the next generation. Thus very good ideas unwittingly introduced into the wiring, though improbable, do become quite widespread in the long run.

This story is quite old and goes by the name of Darwinian evolution. Many people don't like the idea that everything beautiful and marvelous in organic nature should be due to the simple cooperation of reproduction, errors, and selection. This is no problem for us. We have convinced ourselves that beautiful, marvelous, and shrewd machines can be made out of inorganic matter by this simple trick. Moreover, we already know that analysis is much more difficult than synthesis. Where there has been no conscious engineering at all, as in the case of our type 6 vehicles, analysis will necessarily produce the feeling of a *mysterious* supernatural hand guiding the creation. We can imagine that in most cases our analysis of brains in type 6 vehicles would fail altogether: the wiring that produces their behavior may be so complicated and involved that we will never be able to isolate a simple scheme. And yet it works.

Vehicle 7

Concepts

We have already used the word knowledge, even if in a somewhat facetious way, when we discussed the properties of Vehicle 3. And we have just observed how a process akin to Darwinian evolution may incorporate knowledge into machines in a mysterious way, though it is not immediately obvious through what channel the knowledge (about the dangers connected with a cliff) entered the "brain" or in what form it is contained there. In both cases we are referring to fixed, inborn knowledge that, whether right or wrong, belongs to the individual vehicle for better or for worse. This is fine for a set environment but may be catastrophic when the conditions change. Therefore, in a precious vehicle that we love, we should build in mechanisms of adaptation to make it more flexible. Not only will our vehicle then be prepared to meet catastrophic events but it will also be ready to cope with a greater variety of situations and thus be less confined to a particular environment.

We proceed as follows. First, we buy a roll of a special wire, called Mnemotrix, which has the following interesting property: its resistance is at first very high and stays high unless the two components that it connects are at the same time traversed by an electric current. When this happens, the resistance of Mnemotrix decreases and remains low for a while, little by little returning to its initial value.* Now let's put a piece of Mnemotrix between any two threshold devices of a fairly complicated vehicle of type 5. This is a lot of wiring, but the effect is not great at first, due to the high resistance of Mnemotrix. Very little current will spread from an active component to all the other components to which it is connected.

As the vehicle (which is now type 7) moves around and experiences various situations in its environment, some of its Mnemotrix connections will change their strength. Suppose aggressive vehicles in that particular environment are often painted red. Then the sensor for red in our type 7 vehicle will often be activated together with the threshold device that responds to aggressive behavior, and the Mnemotrix wire connecting the two will have its resistance decreased so often that it will not have time to return to its initial value. The consequence is obvious: every time the vehicle senses red, the whole set of movements with which it normally responds to aggressive behavior will be activated. So our vehicle will turn away from its dangerous fellow. The enhanced connection between the components represents what philosophers call ASSOCIATION, the association of the color red with aggression. More generally, we may say a new CONCEPT has arisen in the vehicle: whenever an aggressive vehicle is around, even if it is blue or green, our type 7 vehicle will "see red." As far as we are concerned, this can mean

---

*I don't care if the electricians shudder. They know very well that even if Mnemotrix is not available commercially as a wire, it can be simulated by a simple circuit. And they also know that such things exist in animals' brains. If you want a fairly realistic explanation of Mnemotrix wire, think of a material that changes its conductance as a function of temperature: the current heats the two components connected by Mnemotrix, and the temperature change at the two ends of the connection induces the change in resistance.

only: the vehicle does some of the things it did previously only when it was confronted with the color red.

This process of translating things that happen together in the environment into "complexes" of activity within the vehicles is of such great importance that we ought to familiarize ourselves with it some more. One consequence, we have already seen, is concept formation. When it happens between different categories of things (such as red color and aggression), we prefer to call it association. But it may happen within a single category, say smell, when a number of chemicals dissolved in the air are frequently perceived together, such as burned plastic, lubricating fluid, and battery acid, which are set free when a vehicle is wrecked. So it is justified for surviving vehicles to store the "smell of death" in order to be able, later on, to identify dangerous regions of their environment. This is done by the formation of a new olfactory concept.

Visual concepts may be formed in a similar manner. The straightness of a line in different parts of the visual field, for example, may come to signify the dangerous cliff at the side of the table. And the movement of many objects in different directions may come to represent the concept "region crowded with vehicles." But visual concepts can be treated more efficiently later on when we provide our vehicles with the a priori category of space. For now, we should explore some of the philosophical implications of the process of concept formation.

Let philosophers watch a breed of type 7 vehicles and let them speculate about the vehicles' behavior. One philosopher says: This is all very well, but learning to recognize situations that are of some importance is a fairly trivial performance, especially if it is done the hard way, by reward and punishment. It would be a different matter altogether if these vehicles could form their own concepts in quiet meditation, without an external tutor telling them what is important. But they never will, because abstraction is one of the powers that is unique to the human mind.

But look, says another philosopher, I just watched an ABSTRAC-TION being made by one of these creatures. It was moving around in a crowd of peaceful, unpainted gray vehicles when it met a vehicle painted red that proved to be aggressive; then it met a green vehicle that also proved to be aggressive. When my vehicle met another painted fellow, this one painted blue, it immediately thought that this one was aggressive too. And it turned away in a hurry. This is a true abstraction, the concept of color replacing the individual colors red and green of the original experience. Or if you wish, we can say that a GENERALIZATION has taken place from particular colors indicating danger to the general danger signal "color."

Sure enough, says the third philosopher, but that is not difficult to explain either. It has something to do with the way colors are represented by the activity of the electronic parts in the gadget. Undoubtedly in all the mess of wires there will be one wire that signifies "gray" as the even mixture of all colors. Then there might well be one that signifies "not gray," and that one was active when the red vehicle appeared. So the "not gray" wire had the strongest correlation with aggressiveness, and this was learned. No wonder this "not gray" wire functioned as a danger signal when the blue aggressor arrived.

All right, says the fourth philosopher, but nobody in his right mind ever suspected anything more mysterious behind the "faculty of generalization."

Fine, says I, as long as you admit it.

Space, Things, and Movements

We take the next step in the improvement of our vehicles primarily as a favor to ourselves, to keep things tidy and to make the wiring less cumbersome. But we will find that the introduction of internal maps of the environment is of inestimable value for the vehicles too, making it much easier for them to discover the truth about their environment.

What I mean by a map is this: take a set of photocells, say one hundred of them, but instead of distributing them messily over the surface of the whole vehicle, arrange them in a neat square of ten by ten photocells on the front surface of the casing (figure 11). Now fit a lens on top of the array, making it into a camera. You know that if everything is set correctly, the inverted image of things in front of the vehicle will be projected onto the array. Of course, you cannot pick up a perfect TV picture with just one hundred photocells, but you will get a picture. It will not be scrambled information about the outside world; it will be a representation of the order of things, of their neighborhood relations and, roughly, of the distances between them.

It is easy to make good use of this orderliness. We may build networks of threshold devices that can distinguish among random

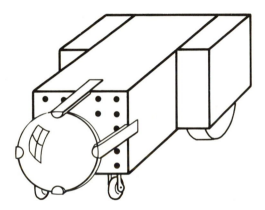

Figure 11

Vehicle 8 with a lens eye.

environments and environments that contain lumps of matter, things that move and ordered structures.

Build yourself an array of threshold devices, each connected to a group of neighboring photocells, say four of them arranged in a square (figure 12). Now as long as the vehicle is surrounded by little insignificant objects or by objects quite far away, all of the photo-cells might see just a few of these things, all in more or less the same numbers. Consequently, the photocells will all become active roughly to the same degree. Even if some photocell accidentally sees a few more things than its neighbors and consequently gives a little more output, the effect will probably be averaged out by the threshold devices, which always add the output of four neighboring photocells. But when a larger object appears in the neighborhood of our vehicle, it will be seen by one or more groups of photocells that are all connected to the same threshold device. This device will be activated much more strongly than the others and thus will func-tion as an *object detector,* of inestimable value for the vehicle.

It might be even more useful to construct a set of *movement detectors* connected with the array of photocells (figure 13). Put the output of each photocell into a *delay,* a device that gives off a signal a little while after it has received one. Nothing's easier than that. A sluggish threshold device will do. Now make a new array of threshold devices. Each is connected with one photocell via a delay device, and with another neighboring photocell located to the right directly, without a delay device. These threshold devices become active only when they receive a signal from both channels. Every time a bright object moves by from left to right, it will elicit a signal in one photocell, which will be stored for a short while in the delay. By the time the object elicits a signal in the neighboring photocell, the delay will give off its signal as well so the two signals will hit the movement detector–threshold device at the same time, making it active. Obviously, a spot moving in the opposite direction will not have the same effect because it will hit the fast threshold device first

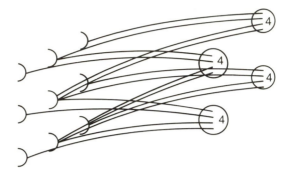

Figure 12

An object detector. Each of the threshold devices on the right responds only when four neighboring sensors arranged in a square are active together.

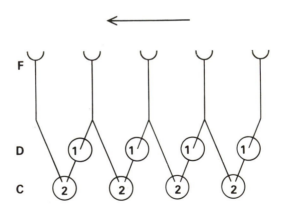

Figure 13

A set of movement detectors (C) for movement from right to left. The threshold devices C become active when they receive input directly from the sensor F to the left, and at the same time receive input indirectly, via a delay element D, from the neighboring sensor to the right.

and the sluggish one afterward—so their output will not coincide at the next level. Thus our movement detectors are directional.

We can of course make different sets of movement detectors for different directions so that no movement will escape the attention of our vehicle. We can also make them for various velocities, or even for objects of various sizes. In order to do this, we first make an array of object detectors, as in figure 12, and connect their outputs in pairs to the movement detectors. Only movement of objects of a certain size, defined by the wiring of the individual object detectors, will elicit activity in the movement detector. We may also proceed the other way around. First we make an array of movement detectors, all tuned to movement of the same velocity in the same direction. Then we take the output of sets of neighboring movement detectors and connect each set to a threshold device, which then acts as an object detector. But this object detector sees an object only as a set of points, all moving in the same direction. This, by the way, is how we humans see certain objects too—such as a cuttlefish moving on the sandy ocean floor, no matter how good the mimicry of the beast.

Another well-known way to make good use of an array of photocells is what is often called *lateral inhibition* (figure 14). Make an array of threshold devices behind the array of photocells. Connect them one-to-one to the photocells, so that each will be activated by light in the corresponding position. Now introduce lateral inhibition: let each active threshold device put a brake on the activity of its neighbors, so that the more it is activated, the more its neighbors are inhibited. You can easily see that there will be an uneven match between neighboring threshold devices receiving different amounts of excitation: the one more strongly excited will put the other one completely out of business. Thus, instead of getting a continuous distribution of activity reflecting all the shades of the environment seen by the photocells, you will get a representation of isolated bright spots. Only in the case of an entirely uniform illumination

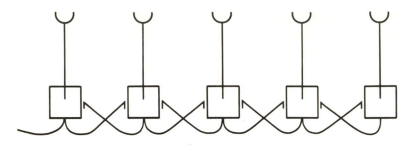

Figure 14

Five threshold devices, excited by that many sensors, each connected to its neighbors by inhibitory connections. Uniform excitation of the whole set will be subdued by the inhibitory interactions, while isolated spots of excitation will stand out.

will all the threshold devices stay at the same level (although there are difficulties at the borders of the array). But in the case of uniform illumination, the threshold devices will also inhibit each other by the same amount. Thus uniformity will be weakly represented, which is all right, for uniformity is uninteresting.

It is quite clear that these tricks, and a number of other tricks that you might invent, are only possible when there is an orderly representation of the "sensory space" somewhere in the body of the vehicle. This need not be 2-dimensional visual space, as in the examples just discussed. It may be 3-dimensional tactile space; we can represent internally, in a 3-dimensional array, all the points that the vehicle touches by means of a jointed arm carrying a tactile sensor. We can also represent 3-dimensional visual space, if we pass the signals from two eyes through a device that performs the sort of computation known as "stereoscopic vision" in human psychology.

We can invent all sorts of bizarre internal spaces which we might use to file in a convenient way the information reaching the vehicle. Two-dimensional visual space combined with one temporal dimension may lead to a representation of all the images, past and present, in a 3-dimensional spatial array within the vehicle. Inspired by some of the things that are known about animal brains, we could also invent a 3-dimensional array for the filing of acoustic information, with one dimension representing the frequency, the second the intensity, and the third the phase of the acoustic signals.

Curiously, when we construct internal spaces for vehicles, we are not even confined by the 3-dimensionality of familiar space that seems to limit our immediate intuitive understanding. It is difficult to imagine solids of more than 3 dimensions, say a 4-dimensional cube or a 5-dimensional sphere. In fact, when we think of an ordinary 3-dimensional cube, we tend to imagine something like a box with 6 square sides. If we want to imagine a 4-dimensional cube, we notice that the sides would have to intersect. But we cannot picture this, so we give up.

On the other hand, it is quite easy to imagine or to draw networks of more than 3 dimensions (figure 15). The drawing shows spheres connected by wires. The network is truly 4-dimensional, since in order to specify the coordinates of one of the balls (or the path that leads from one ball to a certain other ball), you have to indicate how many steps to move in directions x, y, z, and w. If you disregard distance and angles on the drawing (you can't keep them equal on a projection even in the case of a 3-dimensional net), and if you imagine the net continued ad infinitum in all 4 directions, the network will look the same no matter which ball you sit on or in which of the 4 directions you look. Now, you could even build the network, or a piece of it, out of spheres and wires: you would be able to hold in your hands a structure that is intrinsically 4-dimensional, though of course collapsed ("projected") into the 3 dimensions of space in which your hands move. (An architect similarly collapses his buildings into the 2-dimensional space of his drawing board.) You could even sit on your network and squash it into a 2-dimensional felt. It would not matter. A louse finding its way along the wires would still notice the

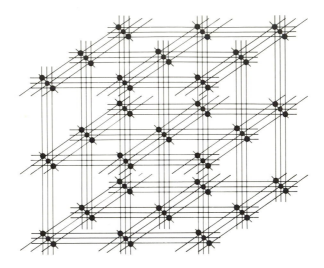

Figure 15
A four-dimensional cube. Each edge is marked by three black dots on a line, connected by a wire.

4-dimensional connectivity, provided it had the necessary mathematical acumen.

The point I want to make is the special virtue of networks as opposed to solids. Once you have decided to represent space by discontinuous, discrete points within the vehicle, you can represent "neighborhood" by means of lines connecting the points. This gives you the freedom to mimic all sorts of spaces, including spaces that a human mind cannot imagine. Can the vehicle imagine such spaces?

We must turn to the philosophers again. Let us ask a philosopher whether Vehicle 8 is endowed with the a priori concept of space, for this is a familiar question to him. Only, in this case the philosopher cannot just close his eyes and look inside himself for an answer. He will have to invent experimental situations in which the vehicle could demonstrate its proper use of an internal representation of space. A simple test: move the vehicle from its present position a certain distance in a certain direction, and then again in another direction. If the place where the vehicle was before had some favorable connotations, it might want to go back. Will it move back exactly the way it came, or will it choose the diagonal, which is the quickest way to get there? If it has an internal representation of 2-dimensional euclidean geometry (that is, if it has 2-dimensional space built in a priori), it will head directly toward the goal.

Now this internal representation of space is something that we could very easily wire into the network within the vehicle. Just imagine a 2-dimensional sheet made of a material which has everywhere the same conductance value for electric currents. This is defined as the current (in amperes) divided by the voltage applied (in volts) for a wire of a certain thickness and a certain length. Now if we apply a voltage difference between two points on the sheet, the current that flows through the material is strongest (the current density, current per cross-sectional area, is highest) along a straight line connecting the two points. If we let one of the two points represent the place where the vehicle is and the other point the place where it wants to go, we can easily construct a device that will determine the best course for the vehicle by way of a simple measurement of current density in different directions on the sheet.

So we would conclude that Vehicle 8 does have the a priori concept of 2-dimensional space. Could Vehicle 8 embody that of 3- and 4-dimensional space as well? To wire an internal representation of 3 dimensions into the vehicle, we could use a block of the same material out of which we made the 2-dimensional sheet, with many electrodes embedded in it to produce voltage differences and measure currents. But for 4 dimensions we already know that we have to resort to 4-dimensional networks, since we are not able to make (or even imagine) 4-dimensional blocks. In principle, this does not make much of a difference. We could still measure shortest distances by the method of current density analysis. We could also use the 4-dimensional network in more complicated ways to let the vehicle show off its built-in a priori concept of higher dimensional space. If the vehicle could talk, we would ask it to rotate in its mind a 4-dimensional cube, let us say 90 degrees, around one of the axes. There are such exercises in human IQ tests, using 2-dimensional pictures of 3-dimensional dice with three sides showing. The three sides are decorated in different ways. The questions are of this sort: is cube A just another view of cube B, C, D, or E? Some humans have trouble with 3-dimensional dice, all with 4-dimensional ones. But a vehicle endowed with a network like the one in figure 15 might very well pass the IQ test for 4-dimensional cubes if the question was posed in a language it could understand.

I can hear myself talking to the philosophers again. The point I am making is that orderly representation of space in a vehicle is more than just convenience of construction. It provides for easy tests of reality. We have seen how easy it is to knit networks that will react to images moving at certain speeds. If these can be taken as images of objects in the world outside, the velocity of the movement of the images will stay between certain reasonable bounds, dictated by the physical laws governing the movement of the objects. In particular, there won't be any movement of infinite velocity; there won't be any sudden displacement. Continuity of movement, no matter at what velocity, is a primary criterion for the physical reality of an object. Also, the continuity and certain regularities of the change of shape of a shadow indicate that the shadow is cast by a solid object. This, too, could be fairly easily detected by a network with 2-dimensional connectivity. And of course identity of shape irrespective of movement (a strong clue for objects keeping a certain geometrical relation with a given vehicle) can also be detected by such networks. We will take up this point again from a different point of view in the next chapter. Here it was sufficient to show that in our vehicle, just as in the physics of relativity, the recognition, or even the existence, of objects is related to the dimensionality of space, internal and external.

Vehicle 9

Shapes

We will improve on our vehicles some more, along the lines outlined in the construction of the preceding brand 8, but with a different intention this time. We will try to furnish our vehicles with a convenient set of ideas referring to the shapes of things, especially to shapes as we see them with our eyes (and as a vehicle sees them if it is equipped with a good camera-type eye).

First of all, if we want to consider shape independently of color and other irrelevant details, we must produce an outline drawing of things in the visual field of the vehicle, as a draftsman would with a pencil. (Webster's dictionary defines shape as "the quality of a thing that depends on the relative position of all points composing its outline or external surface.") This is not very difficult if things stand out clearly against their backgrounds—for instance if these things are birds in the sky or vehicles on a white sheet. We can then use the trick of lateral inhibition, which we have already learned (figure 14). Only sharp boundaries will be passed on to the next level, thereby producing a pure line drawing. If the interior of the figure represented is quite homogeneous, say all black, there will be only the outline or shape.

Let us construct detectors for elementary properties of shape.

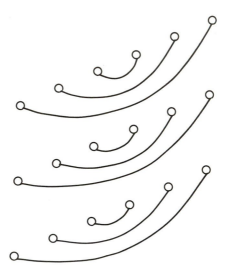

Figure 16
A detector for bilateral symmetry. There is an array of elements onto which an image is projected. Elements symmetrically spaced with respect to the midline enhance each other. There will be a strong activation of the array for bilaterally symmetrical images.

The first property that comes to mind is bilateral symmetry. Its detector is easy to construct and enormously valuable (figure 16). Again we make an array of threshold devices onto which a picture of the external world is projected by means of a suitable camera system (we can filter the picture first through a network with "lateral inhibition" to enhance relevant detail). One half of it receives a picture of the right half of the visual environment, everything to the right of the vehicle; the other half receives a picture of the left half of the world. Now we connect by a wire each pair of threshold devices occupying symmetrical positions on the right and left sides. Through the wire the threshold devices influence one another in such a way that when they both receive input, they become much more active than when only one of them is activated. It is clear now that when the vehicle faces a symmetrical shape (with a vertical axis of symmetry, such as an upright human figure seen from the front or from behind), there will be much more activity in this array of threshold devices than there will be in any other case. For every element excited on one side of the vehicle, its symmetrical element on the other side will also be excited, with the consequent reciprocal enhancement.

Let's not talk about an upright human figure; that introduces an unintended aesthetic aspect. Think only of a world populated by vehicles of the various kinds that we have been building. Up to now we have not talked much about the exterior appearance of our vehicles, although we have implicitly assumed that the vehicles are made of two halves, mirror images of one another: two motors, one on each side, two nostrils, a symmetrical casing like an automobile. Of course such vehicles, seen from the side, are not symmetrical: their sense organs are in front, their motors are in the back, and their prevalent movement is always in the same "forward" direction. Nor are the vehicles symmetrical in the up-down direction if they move around on surfaces, as our vehicles mostly do; for reasons connected with gravitation, there will be wheels (or other instruments of locomotion) on the side of the vehicles facing the ground, the so-called underside.

But there are good reasons for the vehicle to be symmetrical in the direction perpendicular to both the "front-back" and the "up-down" directions—along the axis defined by the pair of concepts "right" and "left." We have seen this early on in the cases of Vehicles 2, 3, and 4, which showed surprisingly lifelike behavior on the basis of paired, very simple, symmetrical connections between two sense organs and two motors. The kind of behavior associated with two symmetrical reins governing the motors is one in which an object is isolated from the environment as a partner in behavior. The vehicle's movements are directed by feedback, either turning the vehicle toward the object or turning the vehicle away from the object.

Consider the first case: feedback that makes the vehicle turn toward the object. An observer might say that our vehicle has that object on its mind or our vehicle pays attention to that object. Well, what if the object is another vehicle? What would the situation look like to that vehicle, and how should it react? Obviously the situation in which a vehicle sees another heading directly toward it, whether in an inquisitive, a friendly, or an aggressive mood, is a special case and well worth special attention. The detector for bilaterally symmetrical shapes, which we have just described, proves helpful here: we may connect it to the output in such a way as to trigger the mechanisms that govern the appropriate reactions to "another vehicle facing me" or "another vehicle having me in mind." (Perhaps one should reactivate the beautiful term "confrontation": fronts coming together, facing each other.) In fact, it is clear that bilaterally symmetrical configurations in a natural world containing only vehicles (and no other man-made objects, such as churches or monuments) would mostly signify just that: a partner in interaction with the observer.

There is a relation between bilateral symmetry in sensory (especially visual) space and the concept of "thou," the pronoun of the second person singular. This has been used by the builders of temples and churches who, by a pointedly symmetrical architecture, evoke the presence of an abstract thou, a partner in conversation always facing the observer. The same principle can be observed in biology: certain flowers, such as orchids, adopt bilaterally symmetrical shapes in order to be accepted as "partners" by insects with detectors keyed to this type of symmetry.

I want you to note that something new and very important has crept into our discussion of a detector with bilateral symmetry. We decided to give our type 9 vehicles a system of connections between corresponding points on their right and left sides. In order to explain how useful such a system would be, we had to invoke not only the external appearance of other vehicles (which our vehicle might meet) but their behavior as well. Things are getting complicated: we are no longer working on individuals taken by themselves but on the members of a community in which there are complicated interactions between vehicles of the same or of different kinds.

Every improvement that we invent for the latest breed of vehicles put in circulation will either force others out of business by a process of Darwinian selection (see Vehicle 6) or make others change their behavior through learning (see Vehicle 7). Of course, this makes it difficult to foresee what will actually work out as an "improvement." Sometimes the net effect will be contrary to what we expect, due to unforeseen reactions of the environment. But certain great inventions will survive all vicissitudes and will be immune to all shrewd defenses. I suspect that the detector of bilateral symmetry, which provides information about "being in someone's focus of attention," belongs to this category. Even in biology with all its complicated interactions between species, the symmetry detector has remained of primary importance. An insect in search of a sexual mate does not really care if it gets occasionally sidetracked by an orchid as long as its symmetry detector serves the right purpose in the majority of cases.

Other insects fall for different kinds of flowers, for those with radial symmetry, like daisies. We can also construct radial symmetry detectors for our type 9 vehicles: these detectors might indicate singularities in the world, sources from which something emanates in all directions. A radial symmetry detector could also be based on the fact that no movement is perceived on approaching a pattern like that of figure 17. The picture remains identical to itself.

A fundamental category of form is periodicity. A repetitive pattern may signify many important situations. It may signify a collection of identical individuals. Then again, a periodic pattern left on the ground may be the track of a vehicle moving by some sort of

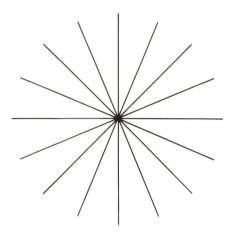

Figure 17

A pattern that is invariant to changes of scale. A vehicle approaching the center of the figure has a constant visual input (provided we make the figure large enough and the lines infinitely thin). The absence of perceived movement may be used as diagnostic for figures with radial symmetry.

periodic stepping mechanism. Or the pattern may be generated by some oscillatory movement in the form of a standing wave—an indication of stored energy. For all these reasons periodic patterns are happenings of great importance in this world; they are just as fundamental as bilaterally symmetrical or radially symmetrical figures. So we should equip our vehicles with detectors for periodicity.

This can be done in various simple ways. For instance, we can give them periodic templates with different spacing and let them match the picture of the environment with the templates by the mathematical process of *cross-correlation*. This is the principle of Fourier analysis. Its technical realization does not require too much ingenuity. Another interesting detector of spatially periodic input is implicitly contained in the network described in the previous chapter as lateral inhibition. We have seen that such an array of threshold devices neglects continuous excitation and enhances contrasts. It gives maximal output for patches of excitation spaced sufficiently far apart so that they won't disturb each other by inhibition. For a periodic pattern, the spacing is determined by the length and strength of the inhibitory connections. If we test the lateral inhibition device with striped patterns, we will notice that it gives the same output no matter how the stripes are oriented if the inhibition works in all directions.

Taken together, vehicles of types 8 and 9 have provided much new evidence for our law of uphill analysis and downhill synthesis. A problem that taxes the minds of psychologists when they deal with real animals or humans, that of inborn concepts, found many solutions when we attacked it from the downhill, synthetic direction. We built very simple homogeneous networks and then discovered that they contain implicit definitions of such concepts as 3-dimensional space, continuous movement, reality of objects, multitude of objects, and personal relation. More and more we are losing our fear of philosophical concepts.

The exercises in synthetic psychology contained in this chapter deal mostly with visual input. It is of course easy to imagine a priori concepts in other categories of input, such as the tactile or olfactory inputs. It is quite elementary to provide the vehicle with detectors of aural periodicity. They would detect various frequencies in the purely time-dependent (nonspatial) input derived from one of the vehicle's ears (microphones). The a prioris of frequency, the so-called resonators, have been basic to human auditory theory for a long time.

Vehicle 10

Getting Ideas

The time has come to sit back and consider the strange variety of vehicles that populate our laboratory. They all go about their business according to certain rules, some of which we understand, because we invented them ourselves, and some we don't, because they emerged from a sort of Darwinian evolutionary process. The objects of their interest are defined by simple properties such as smell and color, or by more abstract properties, such as the periodicity of their coloring or the symmetry of their outline. Formal properties may stand for even more abstract definitions, as we have seen in the case of bilateral symmetry signifying the situation of "somebody having me in mind."

Some of our vehicles seem to move around smoothly, as if attracted and repelled by the sources of various fields of force superimposed on one another. Others appear to make sudden decisions, rousing themselves from a rather phlegmatic condition to take off on isolated ventures, after which they resume their state of rest. The vehicles seem to know their environment rather well, so much so that they are able to reach some objects with closed eyes, so to speak, apparently on the basis of some internalized map on which the object's location is recorded. On the whole, these vehicles are surprisingly smart, especially considering the limited amount of intelligence that we, their creators, have invested in them.

But do they think? I must frankly admit that if anybody suggested that they think, I would object. My main argument would be the following: No matter how long I watched them, I never saw one of them produce a solution to a problem that struck me as new, which I would gladly incorporate in my own mental instrumentation. And when they came up with solutions I already knew, theirs never reminded me of thinking that I myself had done in the past. I require some originality in thinking. If it is lacking, I call the performance at best reasonable behavior. Even if I do observe a vehicle displaying a solution to a problem that would not have occurred to me, I do not conclude that the vehicle is thinking; I would rather suppose that a smart co-creator of vehicles had built the trick into the vehicle. I would have to see the vehicle's smartness arising out of nothing, or rather, out of not-so-smart premises, before I concluded that the vehicle had done some thinking.

But this does not mean that we cannot create vehicles that would satisfy this condition. We shall do this gradually, starting with the problem of *having ideas*. Let us take one of the vehicles of type 7, the ones with the Mnemotrix connections that introduce the effects of experience into the brain. This vehicle has been around for some time and has absorbed a great deal of knowledge about the world. This knowledge takes the form of statistical correlations between elementary events in the vehicle's sensory spaces or statistical correlations between more complex events represented in some threshold devices of its interior (or between elementary events and complex events).

Suppose the vehicle has learned that certain objects, A, B, C, D, are situated near the rim of the table top on which it lives: a broken-down vehicle, a light, a battery, a hill, a supply of screws. It has learned to associate these objects with the concepts "margin of the universe" and "dangerous cliff." On its occasional excursions toward the margin of the universe, it will also have noticed the neighborhood relations among pairs of these objects: the screws are next to the hill, the light next to the battery, and so forth. One day, after enough excursions, the vehicle will suddenly realize that all these paired associations (A next to B, B next to C . . . , Z next to A) make sense if the whole situation is seen as a closed chain. The vehicle now has the idea of a finite bounded universe, with objects A to Z marking the marginal closed line. Once this "image" or "idea" is generated out of individual items of knowledge, it is there to stay. It may, in fact, be immediately recorded on the maps, whose use we have discussed. If so, we will observe that forever after the vehicle moves around much more expertly.

We must be careful, however, not to let the process of acquiring new ideas interfere with the detailed knowledge that our vehicle has assiduously collected and carefully stored in many associative connections during its lifetime. We know that this may happen in humans who are overly dedicated to the development of ideas. They tend to connect many individual cases into general categories and then use the categories as if they were things, losing the potential for categorizing in other ways by remembering each instance.

In the example of the discovery of the margin of the universe, I can see this danger. The idea of a closed chain of objects may be so strong that it keeps the images of these objects permanently active in the vehicle's brain. The consequence is that associations will develop between every object on the margin—and every other object on the margin. The serial order that led to the original idea will thereby be lost or at least submerged in a system of much stronger, massive associations. The way out in our case would be to let the excitation circulate in the closed chain associations. This would strengthen the associations representing the serial order of the objects and would not allow cross-association to develop.

Here are some more examples of ideas that may arise in vehicles. There are coins lying around on the floor in the universe of the vehicles. Some of the coins are decorated with a picture of a human head and others are decorated with a number. One of our vehicles has already learned to recognize and to distinguish the two types of coins. That is, there are distinct patterns of activity, say two different threshold devices becoming active when one or the other kind of coin is seen by the eye of the vehicle. Now one of the coins showing a human head is flipped around by the vehicle—and suddenly it shows the number. This happens again and again until, by the learning process that we have already incorporated in our vehicles, an association is formed: "head, flipping, number." Of course, the association also works the other way around. Once the association is acquired, the vehicle knows that, after adding the action of flipping to the sighting of "number," the picture of the head will be seen. It may also be reinforced by the contrary experience, when the flipping of coins showing the number reveals the head.

We may call the whole complex of head-flipping-number and number-flipping-head the idea of a coin with two faces. It arises in the vehicle although the two faces of a single coin are never seen together. The idea of a coin with two faces can arise even if there are some coins around with human heads on both sides, as long as these coins escape the vehicle during the phase of "getting the idea."

Here's another example. Moving through a garden, a vehicle finds out that flower number one of a row is a source of food, flowers 2 to 7 are not (they are poisonous), flower number 8 is again a source of food and so are flowers 15, 22, and so forth. After a while it may happen that in the brain of the vehicle only one of 7 threshold devices (connected in a circular fashion) always becomes active in temporal coincidence with the finding of a source of food in a flower. This is again "getting the idea": that particular threshold device will be associated with the food finding system—with the consequent advantage of being able to predict sources of food without having to invest much energy in the process of sniffing around. We must suppose, of course, that the time it takes for one threshold device to become active after another has been activated is exactly the same as the time it takes to get from one flower to the next or, better still, that the advancement of activity by one step in the ring of threshold devices is triggered by each flower.

All of this is not complicated in principle but boring to carry out in detail. We rely on the process of Darwinian selection that, starting with the vehicles of type 6, has introduced a great variety of different patterns of connections into the vehicles without our even noticing it (although we do recognize the vehicles' greatly increased complexity of behavior). We can well imagine that the vehicle could get the idea "edible flower" even if the only flowers that were edible were those whose ordinal numbers were square or whose ordinal numbers were prime. There is, however, a complication in the cases of squares and of prime numbers. If these numbers get too large, the vehicle has to perform a long and intricate dance between one flower and the next in order to find out whether the flower's number is square or prime, leaving marks on the earth and retracing them according to complicated rules. We have seen this before, at the end of the chapter on Vehicle 5, which also had its limitations. No such difficulty arises if the vehicle has to find out whether a number is even or odd, or whether a number is a multiple of six or of eleven, as long as the vehicle can count to eleven.

In this chapter we were only interested in the general idea of "getting ideas." Readers who want to know exactly what kind of network of threshold devices is necessary to calculate numbers that are square, or prime or whatever, must read the textbooks of automata theory.

Vehicle 11

Rules and Regularities

Most of you will not yet be convinced that the process of getting ideas as it was described in the previous chapter has anything to do with thinking. It is not surprising, you will say, that occasionally something clicks in the workings of a fairly complicated brain and from then on that brain is able to perform a trick (an algorithm, as some people say) that can be used to generate complicated sequences of numbers or of other images. It is also not surprising that these may occasionally match sequences of events or things in the world of the vehicle.

I will show you that this is just one step in the direction of creating behavior akin to thinking. In the following chapters we will introduce more elements of the thought process, making new vehicles to show new tricks, new types of performance. In the end our vehicles will surprise us by doing some real thinking.

We want to equip Vehicle 11 with a brain about which it can be said—in a more radical way than it could be said about previous editions—that it is a model of the world. We already introduced partial aspects of this model idea, when we talked about the usefulness of internal maps representing external spaces (Vehicle 8), and when we described a learning process (Vehicle 7) that discovers things in the environment and establishes their internal models (called concepts). But this is not enough. These things move around, bang against each other, associate and dissociate, grow and break. We have altogether missed these dynamic aspects up to now.

We will introduce these dynamics by improving on the system of Mnemotrix connections already introduced in the type 7 vehicle. You will remember that these connections between elements in the vehicle's brain were of different strengths and could be made more effective when the elements they connected were often activated together. This turned out to be very convenient, because so many of the facts about the world that are interesting and important to us (and to the vehicles) may be expressed as things or events that tend to occur together. For this reason it is unlikely that we will give up the trick of associative learning in any further development of more refined vehicles.

But we soon discover that there are important pieces of knowledge about the world expressed in a different form: events that do not present themselves at the same time but in succession—pairs of events, of which one is always the first and the other the second, like lightning and thunder, swinging a hammer and hitting the nail, or, in the world of vehicles, meeting a source of food and tasting the food. When we discover a pair of such events, we tend to think that one is the cause of the other, whatever that means. But this may lead to wrong interpretations, for instance when both events are produced by a third hidden event, only with different delays. Most of the time, however, when two events regularly occur in succession, it is no accident. And it certainly is useful for a vehicle to know what to expect when events occur that have important, possibly dangerous, consequences.

We could use our old supply of Mnemotrix wire together with a little electronics to incorporate into the vehicles' brains all those delayed coincidences of events we have been describing. What we want to achieve is a connection between the two internal representatives of an event A and an event B such that, when the representative A is activated by the input, the representative B is activated by the connection, but not vice versa. The connection would then represent the fact that "B often follows A" or, if you wish, the causal tie between A and B. This would force us to do a rather complicated wiring for every such connection. In order not to burden our constructive imagination too much, we prefer to buy a different sort of wire, called Ergotrix, which conducts in one direction only and has an increased conductance when it is interposed between elements that are active in succession within a brief time. We must be careful, of course, to install the wire in the right direction, conducting from the element that tends to be active first to the one that tends to be active second.

Once again we will see to it that all of this happens automatically. Plenty of Ergotrix wire will be installed between as many elements as possible so that whatever sequences occur can be recorded in the system. Of course there will be no lack of opportunity for learning. With all the movement in the world around the vehicle, with all the natural laws operating, and with all the other vehicles displaying fairly regular behavior on the basis of all the tricks that we (or the processes of evolution) have built into them, many sequences of events will repeat themselves and they will be worth learning.

You may ask why we did not use Ergotrix wire in the first place (Vehicle 7) when we first gave our vehicles the capacity to learn, starting with those complexes of properties that frequently occur together because they belong to one "thing." We used the Mnemotrix wire, which is ideal for associations, because it couples elements in a symmetrical fashion; once coupled, each of the properties can recall the other in quite the same way. For each Mnemotrix connection we could have used two Ergotrix wires (one for each direction) to obtain almost the same result. But there are two reasons to leave things as they are.

First of all, we don't want to go back in evolution and change things that have already proved to be convenient, since we might lose some advantage that we have not even realized. (Remember the law of uphill analysis and downhill synthesis: we run the risk of not understanding any longer what we previously put together.) Second, it is probably a good idea to keep the two processes conceptually separated—the associations of elementary properties into things or concepts on one hand and the sequencing of concepts on the other hand, one controlled by the Mnemotrix, the other by the Ergotrix system. The two kinds of learning produce two different kinds of knowledge, like geography and history, or systematic zoology and animal behavior, referring to what kinds of things exist and to how they develop and interact.

If we let our imaginations go and try to work out in detail what kinds of things the Mnemotrix system will discover in a real world, and what kinds of dynamic laws will be incorporated in the Ergotrix system, we soon discover that the two kinds of knowledge are perhaps related more than we had assumed initially for reasons of conceptual convenience. First of all, it would seem that the process of abstracting things from the environment—concept formation at the most elementary level—must occur prior to the process of discovering the dynamic properties of these things. For the laws of successions of events refer to the development and to the combination of things rather than their elementary properties. This is familiar from our own human experience: listening to a new language we want to learn, we must first discover individual words, or roots of words (something like the morphemes in linguistic terminology), before we can even hope to discover the rules that govern their use. Also, in the development of a science it is often apparent how the discovery and denomination of phenomena precedes the definition of the laws of their transformation. Chemistry had to go through a descriptive phase before the physics underlying the variety of substances could be understood. Zoology had to be taxonomic before it was organized by the theory of evolution.

On the other hand, purely descriptive classification is not only boring, it is also potentially misleading. It may lead to the wrong categories when it is not guided by at least the intuition of a theory of the underlying processes. A century of microscopic anatomy has filled the libraries with thousands of beautifully illustrated volumes that are now very rarely consulted because the descriptive categories of the old histology have been largely superseded by the new concepts of biochemical cytology. The example from linguistics that we have just mentioned may well serve to prove the contrary point, with word roots—morphemes—words as the segments of speech that must be learned. While it is true that these chunks of meaning in some languages (largely in English) coincide with acoustically well-defined episodes (the syllables, which the naive listener can recognize), it is certainly true that a better, more general definition of morphemes or words is derived from grammar. Words (I use this term loosely) are the segments of speech that we discover as the ultimate particles of grammar. If we had no idea or no experience of grammar, we might never discover that these are the pieces that are shuffled around to form sentences. We might propose a different, incorrect segmentation of speech, for example, a segmentation into syllables in a language with polysyllabic words. Words become meaningful insofar as they are used in a grammatical system.

In other words, abstracting meaningful chunks from the environment (things, events) and discovering the rules of their behavior are two processes that condition each other and are necessarily interlaced, like the learning of the vocabulary and the learning of grammar in a language course.

Coming back to Vehicle 11, it seems like a good idea to let the discoveries of the Ergotrix system influence the learning process in the Mnemotrix system, on whose initial abstractions it in turn depends. I don't want to work this out in detail, but something like the following scheme would clearly be possible. We have already described the conditions for the strengthening of an Ergotrix wire. These conditions are fulfilled when an element, say a threshold device, at one end of the wire becomes active shortly before another element becomes active at the other end. We have also seen that it is mostly groups of such elements, strongly interconnected and representing "things," that become active in succession. Now let's introduce the rule that whenever the Ergotrix wires become strengthened, the Mnemotrix wires within each of these groups will also become strengthened.

Thus concepts are established in the vehicle especially when they appear in regular sequences. How would this look to us? We would notice, observing the apparently erratic behavior of a vehicle in its world, that the vehicle displays particularly well defined reactions to events that are known to have consequences. Take, for example, a vehicle approaching an obstacle at high speed. We would not be surprised to see the vehicle promptly react to its perception of the danger of a collision. Similarly, Vehicle 11 will quickly remember which of its own behavior patterns regularly and quickly elicit a reaction from other vehicles. We observe that after an initial learning period Vehicle 11 will either produce these behavior patterns frequently or pointedly avoid them. It will use them as signals. It will also learn those signals that regularly precede certain behavior patterns of other vehicles. After a while Vehicle 11 will react to these premonitory signals just as it reacted, before the learning, to the behavior that regularly followed the signals.

But it would take prolonged observation to notice this particular aspect of learning in the vehicles. As a matter of fact, we might not have suspected it if we had not introduced a piece of our own philosophy into the construction of these vehicles. As our brain children become more efficient, we notice that the "law of uphill analysis and downhill synthesis" becomes more and more compelling. For the time being, take the message in this form: since you were not satisfied with the first meager showing of intelligence in our vehicles, we started adding a few more tricks, hoping that they would convince you a little more. The first trick we tried was the coding of the environment in those terms that yield a maximum of correlations and logical structure, in other words, in the most meaningful terms.

Vehicle 12

Trains of Thought

At this stage, if you want to be critical, it is easy for you to maintain that up to now you have not discovered anything in our vehicles that goes beyond ordinary learning. True, these creatures seemed to become more and more able to deal with the adversities of their environment, not only by a process of Darwinian selection but also by active assimilation of information from the world. But thinking is different. It is a process that can go on for a long time, as everyone who has done some conscious thinking knows. Thinking can be observed in other people as well, when we get verbal or nonverbal evidence for a succession of mental states that are guided by some criterion of plausibility or logic—mental states that reflect the exploration of various blind alleys and eventual arrival at a result. Sometimes we seem to notice such mental operation even in a monkey or in a dog. But not yet in a vehicle.

The possibility of sustaining long successions of distinct brain states for the purpose of exploring knowledge already incorporated in the brain is what we will introduce in a new brand of vehicle, which we will call Vehicle 12.

First a remark on pathology. All the later vehicles, beginning with type 7, are in constant danger of running into a condition quite analogous to epilepsy (which is also one of the most common forms of derangement of animal brains). The strengthening of the connections between the elements of the brain, which is at the basis of associative learning, embodies the danger of reciprocal activation beyond control. In a population of elements in which excitatory connections abound, if the number of active elements reaches a certain critical level, chances are the remaining ones will also become activated. These elements, in turn, keep the first set active. A maximal condition of activity is then established and maintained until the supply of energy is exhausted. This maximal activation makes no sense in terms of the information ordinarily handled by the brain, which is keyed to patterns of partial activation of the elements. Necessarily the result is disorderly, ineffective behavior. There are various ways of dealing with this danger, and I propose the following for our vehicles.

Let every threshold device in the vehicle's brain be touched by a special wire through which we can control its threshold. If we set the thresholds high, the threshold devices will become active only when they are very strongly activated by the input they receive from other threshold devices or from the sensors. For a lower threshold, less input will suffice. So if we watch the operation of the brain— and in particular the total amount of activity in it—we can always prevent an attack of epilepsy by raising all the thresholds. If there is not much activity, we can lower all the thresholds and thereby encourage the circulation of activity through the brain. It is of course quite easy to let this happen automatically. All we need (figure 18) is a box that receives as its input the number of active brain elements at that moment and calculates appropriate thresholds, which it then sets for the whole brain. In real life, the input for this threshold control device might be the rate of change of the number of active elements, in order to give it an opportunity to foresee the catastrophic explosion of activity before it happens. But

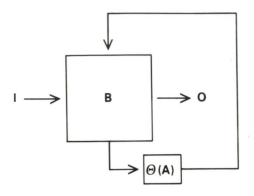

Figure 18

B is the brain, which receives input I and elaborates an output O. At the same time it signals the level of activity A in its interior to a special box that calculates appropriate thresholds Θ for the elements in B.

for purposes of illustration it will suffice if the threshold control device works just on the amount of activity in the brain.

The effect of this global negative feedback on the activity of a vehicle's brain is illustrated in figure 19, which shows the number of active elements as a function of the number of active elements a moment earlier. When the activity is low, it will again be low at the next moment. (For very low excitation, there may even be a tendency for the activity to die out, since a minimum density of active elements in the brain is required to activate the next set of elements, but this is not shown in figure 19.) For very high levels of excitation—that is, for a very large number of active elements—we may imagine that the thresholds are immediately set so high that the activity will drop to a very low level at the next moment. Intermediate levels of activity will lead to maximum activity at the next moment (see the middle part of the curve in figure 19). Later on we will come back to this curve, which has interesting philosophical implications. First let us watch the operation of a brain that con-

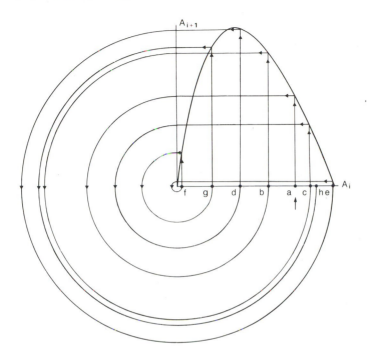

Figure 19
The function describing the next number of active elements A_{i+1} given the present number of active elements A_i. It can be seen by iteration (follow the lines starting from the arrow near a) that the states of a brain controlled by such a rule are quite unpredictable.

tains many learned associative connections while it is being controlled by the feedback of a threshold control device.

We have already noticed that the vehicle's brain has a tendency to explode into fits of activity because of the abundance of reciprocal activation between its elements, a situation reminiscent of the chain reaction in a block of uranium. But most of these explosions, if everything works out the way we have planned, should take place within limited groups of elements that are tied together by particularly strong associative connections. Such sets of elements arise as "concepts" representing things or events that have often presented themselves in the environment.

Let one such thing appear in the sensory space of Vehicle 12. The explosion of activity will happen in the corresponding set of threshold devices responsible for that concept. This implies an increase of the number of active elements in the brain, and the threshold control device will immediately react to it by raising all the thresholds. A moment later many elements that were previously active will be silent. But the elements pertaining to the concept in question are likely to stay active. This is because the strong reciprocal connections within the set, once activated, guarantee a very high level of excitation for each element of the set. This level is so high that the activity of the elements may survive the raising of the thresholds. Thus the first interesting effect of our recent innovation is the focusing of individual concepts—of patterns that have their own internal consistency—at the expense of background activity. We greatly appreciate this effect in a well-functioning human brain, where it is often called the FOCUSING OF ATTENTION.

But there is more. You remember that we have installed not only Mnemotrix wire for concept formation but also Ergotrix wire, which represents within the brain the relation of temporal succession, of consequence or causality. Thus the elements now active in the lone surviving concept after the automatic raising of the thresholds also have some Ergotrix wires attached to them. These Ergotrix wires lead to the elements that have often been activated after the concept in question, the consequences of the active concept, so to speak. Obviously, there will be more than one possible next step for all but the most determined situations.

So we must ask ourselves how the vehicle's brain finds the concept that follows the one it presently holds. The choice, it turns out, is quite automatic. Among all the elements activated by the present concept through the Ergotrix wires, there will be some groups strongly connected by Mnemotrix wires because they again form concepts. These groups will of course ignite with particular alacrity because the internal connections within each group will provide an explosive kick to the activation from external sources, that is, from the active concept. Now you can see what will happen. The threshold control, alarmed by all this growth of activity, will quickly raise the thresholds, smothering most of the activity and leaving only the most resistant group of elements activated. As we have already seen, this will be the group with the strongest reciprocal connections. In terms of concepts we may put it this way: the next concept, among all the concepts that are possible consequences of the present one, will be the most consistent or familiar one—the one most strongly established by experience.

Note that with all these budding and growing explosions the thresholds have been raised above the level at which they were set for the previous concept. It is therefore very likely that the previous concept will be extinguished. So the system will not swing back into its former condition but will end up with a different concept. This new concept will have its own consequences embodied in Ergotrix wires. And these will again materialize in a new concept by way of the sequence of events that we have just described. The process will continue as long as you wish or as long as the chain of concepts does not lead back to the concept from which it started.

The upshot is something very much akin to thinking, to that process so familiar to our introspection, where images appear in succession according to rules reflecting the relations between the things they stand for. This process goes on in our minds when we try to figure out the best way to get from one point to another in a familiar city by letting our imagination produce successions of street corners (or other landmarks) whose relations of geographical proximity we have experienced. It is also one of the tricks we use to determine the consequences of possible moves in a game of chess, or the consequences of some statement in a discussion. This chaining of internal states is exactly what we planned to introduce into the brain of Vehicle 12 to make its meditations look more lifelike, more like our own, not only in the time they take but also in the unforeseen routes they can follow.

There is an important property that the brain of Vehicle 12 shares with the brains of our fellow men. Consider again the curve of figure 19, which shows the number of active elements as a function of the number of active elements a moment earlier. The exact shape of the curve is not very important, as long as it has a maximum and cuts the diagonal $(A_i = A_{i+1})$. Start with a certain value a on the abscissa and find the ordinate of the next value b on the curve. Put that value b again on the abscissa and find c, and so on. You will be surprised to find that the succession of values a, b, c . . . does not seem to follow any rules and is in general quite unpredictable. Now you will remember that figure 18 describes the effect of threshold control on the activity of the brain of Vehicle 12. We may take a, b, c . . . as the number of active elements in the brain in successive moments of time. If there are very few elements, the succession will by necessity become repetitious after a short while. But for a fairly large brain the succession will be truly unpredictable to an observer, for any practicable stretch of time.

I hope you realize what this means. If you could observe the inner workings of the vehicle's brain, say, by watching light bulbs connected to the threshold devices, and these light bulbs lit up every time the corresponding element became active, you could not even predict how many lights would light up in the next moment, let alone what kind of pattern they would form. (For any given number there are of course many constellations with that number of active elements!) At this point we should again invite our philosophers to comment.

I would claim that this is proof of FREE WILL in Vehicle 12. For I know of only one way of denying the power of decision to a creature—and that is to predict at any moment what it will do in the future. A fully determined brain should be predictable when we are informed about its mechanism. In the case of Vehicle 12, we know the mechanism, but all we can prove is that we will not be able to foresee its behavior. Thus it is not determined, at least to a human observer.

I know what the philosophers will reply. They will say that although this may look like free will, in fact it is not. What they have in mind when they use that term is the real power of decision, a force outside any mechanical explanation, an agent that is actually destroyed by the very attempt to put it into a physical frame.

To which I answer: whoever made animals and men may have been satisfied, like myself, a creator of vehicles, with something that for all intents and purposes looks like free will to anyone who deals with his creatures. This at least rules out the possibility of petty exploitation of individuals by means of observation and prediction of their behavior. Furthermore, the individuals will themselves be unable to predict quite what will happen in their brains in the next moment. No doubt this will add to their pride, and they will derive from this the feeling that their actions are without causal determination.

Vehicle 13

Foresight

And indeed—following up the last sentence of the previous chapter—it may be said that the internal rumblings of Vehicle 12 are at least aimless, if not random, constrained as they are only by the rules of plausibility stored in the vehicle's memories (Mnemotrix and Ergotrix) but not determined by them.

I am sure that most of you will not believe that "aimless succession of images" is an accurate description of what goes on in your minds most of the time. You will not be impressed by our vehicles as long as there is no evidence of some purpose guiding their behavior and some direction in their thinking. These are virtues we are pleased to see in our children. Why shouldn't we try to modify our brain children, the vehicles, in this direction? It won't be difficult in principle, and it means a lot to those philosophers who like to think that goal-directed behavior is the one property that gives living beings their very special status within the physical universe.

There are two aspects of goal-directed behavior we must consider. First, the goal lies in the future. For instance, the eating of the mouse is the goal determining the movements of the cat now. We have the special case of an event defined for a later time having earlier effects, quite contrary to the effects that we are used to considering in physics. Second, the goal is desirable by its very definition. We cannot talk about goals without first getting straight the concepts of good and bad.

Let us take the first problem first, that of acting toward the future or in accordance with an event in future time. This is obviously nonsense if we take it to mean an action that is now a consequence of something that will happen only in the future. However, it is an entirely different matter—and it does make sense—if we take it to mean an action that is a consequence of something we expect to happen in the future, since that expectation may well be available before the action is planned. There is no violation of the law of causality in this. All we need is a mechanism to predict future events fast enough so that they will be known before they actually happen.

There are of course safe predictions—and others that are not so safe. We have no problem predicting the future of a rolling stone once it is on its way down the slope of a hill. But it is not so certain whether a dog will leave its comfortable pillow when it is shown a piece of cake. Other motions are practically unpredictable, like that of a child playing in the middle of the street. Yet the principle of the prediction is very similar in these cases. We have seen enough rolling stones and hungry dogs that the perception of one situation immediately brings to mind its consequences. Stored sequences of events are all we need for prediction, together with a mechanism forcing them to speed up in the reproduction when necessary, for example, in dangerous situations. Complications may arise when several different predictions are approximately equally likely. In a good prediction there must be the possibility of predicting various outcomes, given a certain situation, and of keeping the various outcomes in mind in parallel. This is what we do when we drive through a street where children are at play.

Now we want to incorporate prediction into the vehicles of type 13. Clearly, the prerequisites are all there in previous types of vehicles. We were careful to reproduce inside the vehicles' brains many rules and regularities that govern the world. This way we could speak of the vehicles' brains as models of the world, as miniature editions of external, public space. Their brains were populated with patterns of activity that mimicked the activities of real objects in their environment. We noticed that these brains (as models of the environment) really came to life only when the dynamic aspects of the world were also represented, so that a given functional state of the elements of the brain would evolve into the next state according to the same rules that make the world evolve from one moment to the next. We did this by using Ergotrix wire, which activates the elements of the brain in the same order as the sequence of events to which they correspond. And we implicitly assumed that the Ergotrix wires would be trained to reproduce sequences of activation at the same pace as the original occurrence of the sequences of events. But this is a somewhat gratuitous assumption: the Ergotrix wires could work faster, or slower, than the sequences that are impressed upon them. Let them reproduce the sequences at a more rapid pace and you will have a brain that works as a predictor (figure 20).

We want to take a closer look at what goes on in a vehicle equipped with such a predictor. Remember that the threshold devices in the brain are under the influence of two kinds of input: first, directly or indirectly (via interposed filters) from the senses and, second, from one another. Only the latter kind of influence is mediated by Mnemotrix or Ergotrix wires. Consider a certain state: the vehicle in quiet contemplation of the world, the threshold control at rest, and the thresholds set high enough so that only a few ideas stand out over the background. (These ideas are of course represented by groups of active threshold devices with their Mnemotrix cross-connections.)

The evolution of the vehicle's mental state may be affected in three ways. First, meditation. Even if the brain is at equilibrium, with the thresholds fixed, it cannot be entirely at equilibrium be-

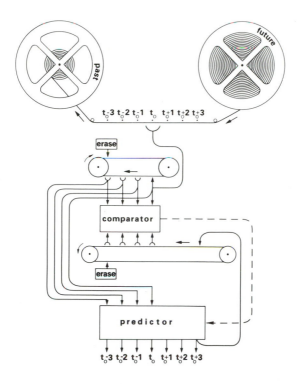

Figure 20

A predictor with some auxiliary equipment. The flow of life is represented by the film (or tape) being unwound from the reel marked *future* and ending up on the reel marked *past*. Only one moment of time, t_o, is available as input to the machine. The input is stored, however, for three units of time on the endless tape of a short-term memory. From there both the present input and the content of the short-term memory are relayed to the predictor which computes the future three units of time ahead. The predictor contains statistical information about the past embodied in the Ergotrix wires in its interior. The prediction for $t_o + 3$ is stored on another short-term memory until it is ready to be compared, by a special comparator, to the real input t and to the input three units of time back. (This depth in time of the comparator is desirable in order to assess the dynamic properties of the predictor.) The comparator in turn emits signals that may modify the predictor or switch it off (broken arrow).

cause the Mnemotrix connections between the active elements will slowly grow in power, the longer the idea is on. But this may not be apparent for a while, unless new elements are recruited to make the idea more ponderous, thereby upsetting the equilibrium and making the brain go on a thinking tour, as we have already seen (Vehicle 12).

Second, things may happen in the environment. The vehicle's mental state will change according to new input from its sensors. The transition from one state to the next will be aided by the Ergotrix wires in the case of a sequence of events that has occurred before, but the Ergotrix connections are too weak by themselves to effect the transition without the help of the sensors' input.

Third, the sensors may signal a condition of the environment that has always evolved in a certain way in the past. The Ergotrix connections in this case will be very strong. And the next state of the vehicle's brain will be entirely determined by them. As a result the vehicle will be blind to the real input that follows. Most of the time this will not hurt the vehicle because the sequence of events will be the same as it has been in the past.

But occasionally the rare event happens and the input clashes with the internal prediction. This will result in a garbled condition that cannot develop further in any coherent way. We want to avoid this, especially in view of the fact that discrepancies between reality and expectations are interesting and should be analyzed in detail. Eventually we would like to provide the vehicle with a device that is turned on by just these discrepancies and amends the system of rules used for the prediction, so that the vehicle will know better the next time it meets the same situation.

First, we provide the vehicles with two separate representations of the environment, one in the predictor, the other in an equally large ensemble of elements that receive only the fresh input from the sensors and do not elaborate on it. These two half brains are connected point to point to each other, so that the discrepancies between their states of activity can be detected as easily as the differences between two drawings if you hold them one on top of the other against the light. The technical realization is easy. Say the two half brains are connected by inhibitory connections between corresponding points. There won't be much activity if the two patterns of activation are exactly equal, because of the reciprocal inhibition. But if one of the two representations contains some activity not present in the other, this will stand out strongly.

We want our vehicles to be imaginative, but mainly realistic. That's why in the case of conflicting information we want to take the information from the realistic half brain more seriously than that from the predictor. We may incorporate a rule: when in doubt, believe the sensors. And we do this by introducing a mechanism that simply turns off the predictor in cases of conflict. But we want to go one step farther; we want to educate the predictor to make it more realistic. This is not as easy as it may sound. Remember that the event in the environment that caused the predictor to make the wrong prediction belongs to the past by the time the clash between the two half brains reveals the mistake.

Thus we want something like short-term memory (figures 20, 21), a third representation of the environment lagging behind the other two, so that, if necessary, the past is available at any time a few steps back. Such a mental echo is not difficult to incorporate in the vehicle's brain. Just connect every element of the sensory half brain with another element that becomes active one unit of time after the first, and with yet another set of elements that becomes active two units of time later, and you have an efficient short-term memory.

Now with a few additional pieces of equipment, we can greatly improve the predictor by making it more flexible and open to new experiences. We do not worry about occasional wrong predictions, especially if the mistakes are not fatal ones. Knowledge is incorporated all the time in the Mnemotrix and Ergotrix connections, and

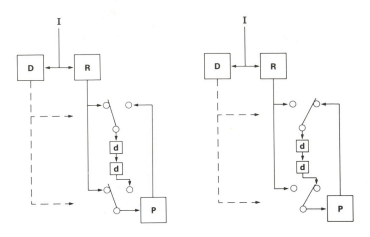

Figure 21

Learning by internal repetition of one-time events. I is the input. D is the Darwinian brain which emits judgments on the desirability of the input and sets two switches accordingly (through the broken arrows). On the left: normal operation, with the Darwinian brain quiescent. The realistic brain R feeds the predictor P and also an open chain of two delay elements d. On the right: the Darwinian brain D signals emotional input. The two switches are thrown to the right, the predictor is no longer fed by the realistic brain but receives the contents of the two delay elements d to which in turn it gives output. The information preceding the emotion reverberates through the predictor and the delay elements until the Darwinian brain calms down again and sets the switches to the normal position.

the statistical knowledge about the world they represent is never complete (by its very statistical nature!). But this piecemeal learning may not be sufficient when the one occasional deviation from the statistics is a very important one (in the good or in the bad sense). Say, for example, that most of the time green vehicles display peaceful behavior, but there is an occasional green vehicle whose aggressiveness is particularly vicious. It would be wrong to associate the property "99% peaceful" with the color green and to react indifferently to the sight of green, since sooner or later an encounter with the green maverick is bound to take place and the victim must be on the defensive. It is better then to give special weight to the rare but decisive experience and to consider green vehicles as generally bad.*

How is this done? We are talking about "good" and "bad" as if these concepts were easy to define. Of course they are not, but there is a way out of this difficulty. Remember the vehicles of our earlier models. They were fairly simpleminded compared to the ones we are now developing, but they were efficient. The type 6 vehicles, which underwent a process of Darwinian selection, know one thing for certain: the avoidance of danger and the search for advantage. And they know this even though no one (neither the vehicles' builders nor the vehicles themselves) has any idea of a definition of good or bad. The type 6 vehicles simply move forward toward good things and back away from dangerous things. But this is all we need.

Catch one of those Darwinian vehicles of type 6, take away its motors, and you have a detector for good and bad. The wire that went to the forward motor signals "good" and the wire that went to the backward motor signals "bad." So we can incorporate the brain of Vehicle 6 into the brain of Vehicle 13 and thereby provide it with important, ancient, intuitive knowledge.

We can now put the pieces together. Short-term memory, two steps back in time for everything that happened, is already there. The predictor is there. A switch that momentarily turns off the

*I hope you remember that we are only talking about little machines. It would be wrong to cite the usefulness of one-instance learning in vehicles as a justification for prejudice and superstition in human behavior. We do have vastly more complex brains that enable us to make the diagnosis of good and bad independent of superficial markers such as the shape or the color of the casing.

predictor in the case of a conflict between prediction and reality is also there. The Darwinian evaluator is ready to signal particularly sinister or joyous events. The new trick: figure 21.

Whenever the Darwinian evaluator D signals an unpleasant turn in the real course of events, or a very pleasant one, the predicting half brain P is disconnected from the input it normally receives from the realistic (sensory) half brain, R. Instead the predicting half brain receives its input from the short-term memory two steps back. So it will go again through the two instants preceding the important happening. At the same time its output is connected to the input of the short-term memory. So it will receive over and over again via the short-term memory the succession of the two events, a and b, until the Darwinian evaluator D has calmed down and everything is switched back to normal.

The net effect is that successions of events leading to strongly emotional consequences are incorporated firmly in the Mnemotrix-Ergotrix system even if they occur only rarely. The internal reverberation set up by the Darwinian evaluator artificially makes up for their low frequency and turns them into high-frequency events in the inner workings of the brain.

We may relax now and observe Vehicle 13 in action. Its power of prediction is quite apparent when it follows a moving object around, say another vehicle carrying a source of attraction. When the object temporarily disappears behind an obstacle, Vehicle 13 will head toward the place where it is likely to show up again. We also notice more peculiar properties. For no obvious reason, Vehicle 13 seems to avoid certain places and vehicles in its environment, and it seems to have an irrational affection for some other places and vehicles. If we watch it long enough, we may find out that there are indeed reasons for these idiosyncrasies. The vehicle may associate a one-time event with this or that place or vehicle, and act accordingly. Vehicle 13 remembers facts much as we do, individual facts and events of its past experience. This remembering is different from the memory we have considered before, which consisted in the molding of behavior according to the unchanging rules and regularities of the environment, perceived through the statistics of many individual events. The vehicles of type 13 derive their experiences from rare but important happenings. They will be quite different, one from the other, because each vehicle builds up its own character based on the particular experiences of its early life.

Vehicle 14

Egotism and Optimism

As time goes on, we grow affectionate toward the diversified crowd of our vehicles, from the very simple ones to the more complex models displaying interesting social interactions and sometimes quite inscrutable behavior. We can play with them, we may get to know them personally (and they may get to know us), we can tease them, test them, teach them tricks, and let them love or fight each other. We do not feel, however, that they show any personality, not even the most complex ones of type 13. It is difficult to say what we mean by that.

Perhaps we would accept them more readily as partners if they gave more convincing evidence of their own desires and projects. We notice that our fellow men usually seem to be after something, when they go about their business or when we converse with them. Dealing with people is interesting because of the challenge their continuous internal scheming seems to provide. The system of desires we suspect behind their scheming may be part of what we call the personality. It may be the lack of just such projects that we notice in our vehicles. We cannot help feeling that they are driven by necessity rather than drawn by goals—in spite of all the efforts we put into them, in spite of special mechanisms that are apt to abolish lowly forms of causality, and in spite of the predictor that seems to draw motives from a future state of the world.

Once we have noticed this, we can of course, in a last creative effort, endow a new kind of vehicle, our last, Vehicle 14, with a certain amount of systematic egotism, with a touch of the pleasure principle, in order to make it look more like our fellow humans. We proceed as follows.

Remember that our more sophisticated vehicles already have built into them many components that come in handy for this new project. With the introduction of the Ergotrix wires (Vehicle 10) prediction became one of the vehicles' mental habits. In Vehicle 13 the updating of the predictor was greatly improved by a mechanism giving great weight to rare but important events. This was achieved by incorporating into the brain of Vehicle 13 another, more primitive, Darwinian brain that contributed all the ancient information about good and bad things its ancestors had accumulated through the generations.

Still earlier, we had noticed (Vehicle 12) that the succession of mental states dictated by the Ergotrix connections was essentially random and quite unpredictable (perhaps even unpredictable as a matter of principle because of the peculiar mathematical property we associate with the function of figure 19). The randomness of the decisions made by Vehicle 12 in part reflected the statistical nature of the knowledge incorporated in the Ergotrix connections and the continuous updating of this knowledge by an ongoing learning process. It also depended on the very nature of the process that makes the brain swing from one state of activity to the next during alternate episodes of raising and lowering the thresholds, automatically imposed by the mechanism of threshold control. We will now give this process an optimistic slant so that the pump of thoughts in the brain of the vehicle will produce a succession of more and more pleasurable mental images. We will convince ourselves in the end that such optimism not only leads to nice dreams but also has objectively favorable consequences.

We will assume that most of the time the uncertainty as to the next state, given a certain state of activity, is not only an uncertainty for the observer but an inherent uncertainty in the sense that the predictor points toward (at least) two states that are equally likely as a continuation of the present state of the brain (and therefore of the world). Such a dilemma in previous vehicles might have been decided by a random element built into the brain (for example, by a Geiger counter making its decisions on the basis of whether or not it was hit by a cosmic ray within the last tenth of a second). But from now on we will impose the following rule for Vehicle 14: when choosing among several equally likely next brain states, choose the most pleasing one.

You have already guessed how we want to achieve this. We hold the present state for a short time (no problem, short-term memory is already there) while the predictor is allowed to go quickly through its various predictions. At the same time the built-in Darwinian evaluator is asked to evaluate these predictions for their favorable or unfavorable aspects. It will in general come up with different values for the different predictions. When this is done, the predictor quickly goes once again through its predictions and stops at the prediction with the highest score for pleasurableness. This is then the next state of the brain.

We don't need more than that. We may put the vehicles back on the table and meditate about their behavior. A superficial observer, or an impatient one, will not notice anything special. We, as creators of vehicles and experienced observers of their behavior, do notice subtle changes in our latest perfected brain children. We know their tastes: we have ample opportunity to see which sources of stimuli, which situations and which other vehicles they are attracted by and which they avoid. Their reactions to these things in the past were quite direct and easily observable when the object was in the vicinity of the vehicle. Distant sources and situations did not seem to affect them much.

Now it is different with type 14 vehicles. They move through their world with consistent determination, always clearly after something that very often we cannot guess at the outset—something that may not even be there when the vehicle reaches the place it wants to get to. But it seems to be a good strategy, this running after a dream. Most of the time the chain of optimistic predictions that seems to guide the vehicle's behavior proves to be correct, and Vehicle 14 achieves goals that Vehicle 13 and its predecessors "couldn't even dream of." The point is that while the vehicle goes through its optimistic predictions, the succession of internal states implies movements and actions of the vehicle itself. While dreaming and sleepwalking, the vehicle transforms the world (and its own position in the world) in such a way that ultimately the state of the world is a more favorable one.

We observe at some stage how one of the vehicles of type 14 is waiting for another vehicle to appear. This other vehicle carries a very appealing source which Vehicle 14 intends to tap. It seems to be waiting impatiently, since every now and then it performs the motions that are associated with the tapping, as if by anticipating its own behavior in the presence of the desired event, it could accelerate the event's occurrence. "This is very human," we say. "Haven't we all felt an urge to run to the door long before the doorbell rings, when waiting impatiently for a beloved friend?" Indeed, it is aberrant behavior dictated by a very subjective law of causality, but it does seem to reflect a basic attitude of humankind, this irrational belief in the effectiveness of one's own actions.

This portfolio of vehicles, some placidly at rest, most madly careening over the landscape of the artist Maciek Albrecht's imagination, illustrates only a few of the many marvelous "creatures" inspired by Valentino Braitenberg's text.

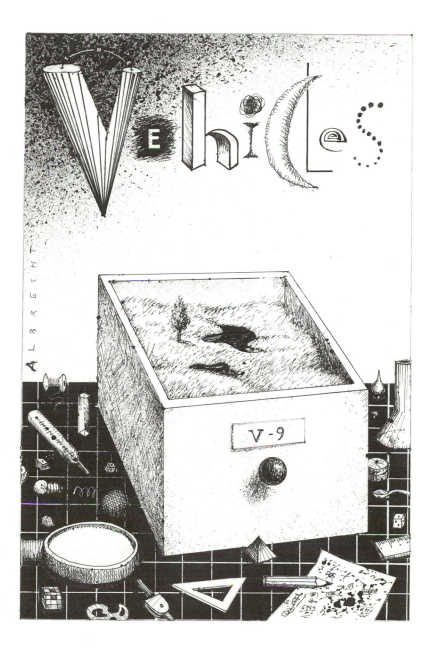

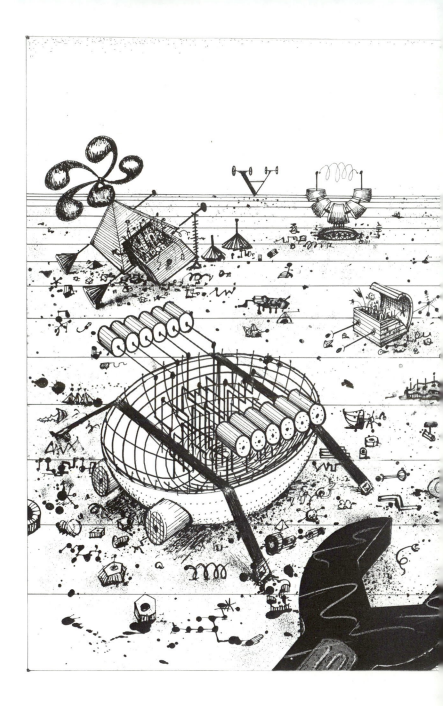

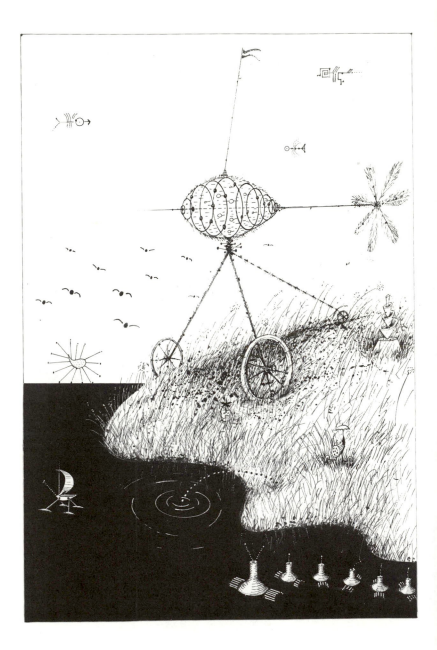

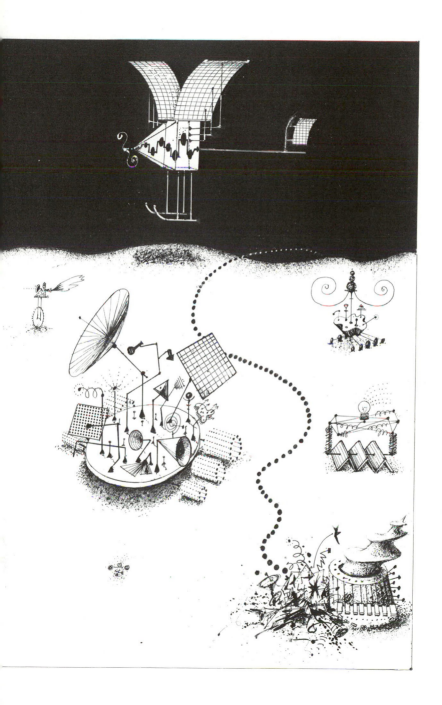

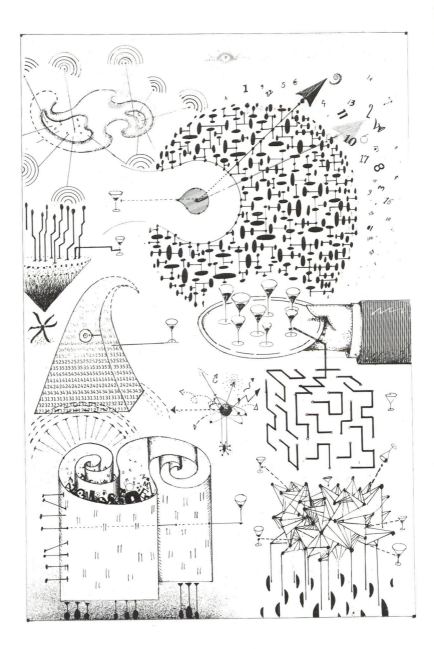

Biological Notes
on the Vehicles

The preceding fantasy has roots in science. I will now sketch a few facts about animal brains that have inspired some of the properties of our vehicles, and their behavior will then seem less gratuitous than it may have seemed up to this point. I have been directly or indirectly involved in most of the research I shall mention. These notes should not be taken as a treatise on brain science but as a series of disconnected and quite personal essays.

The virtues of crossed connections
(Vehicles 2, 3, and 4)

Vehicles 1 to 4, the early ancestors of the whole breed, spring from an attempt to understand that very curious basic fact of brain science, the crossed representation of the world in the (vertebrate) brain. The general principle is apparent in the projection of visual space onto the brain. A million or so fibers of the two optic nerves carrying signals from both eyes toward the brain cross each other in such a way as to represent in the left brain an image of everything to the right of the animal and vice versa in the right brain. Just how many fibers of the right eye actually see points of the right half of the visual field is a question that obviously depends on the position of the eyes in the head. In a frog or a mouse the right eye looks to the right and the left eye to the left, but in a cat or a monkey—animals with forward looking eyes like ourselves—each eye sees almost equal portions of the right and left halves of the world. The fibers in the optic nerves in each of these cases exactly follow the rule that everything from the right world goes into the left brain and vice versa, which makes for a rather more complicated scheme in the case of eyes pointing forward. Incidentally, the same rule is valid for the sense of touch, where again information from the left half of the skin is relayed to the right half of the brain and vice versa. The motor system is also crossed: the nerve cells whose activity is most evidently associated with a certain motor act are on the side of the brain opposite to that of the limb being moved. Thus there is some justification for saying that the two halves of the world are represented in the opposite halves of the brain. But why should this be so?

Since it was first discovered, the fact of crossed projection has presented a puzzle, and various explanations have been attempted. These have ranged from simple mechanical interpretations to elaborate constructions involving arguments about image processing within the central nervous system. At the simplest level it has been argued that the abundance of crossed fiber bundles makes the brain mechanically more stable, by a lacing or weaving effect. Another very general argument places the origin of fiber crossings in the transition from a primitive (hypothetical) brain with spherical symmetry to the bilaterally symmetrical brain of most animals (figure 22). It is argued that as a median plane becomes defined in this transition, we may rename the connections, initially supposed to be random, as crossed and uncrossed: the longest and therefore most important fiber bundles will be the ones that cross the median plane. Apart from weak points in this argument, it should be valid for invertebrate as well as vertebrate brains. But while crossed pro-

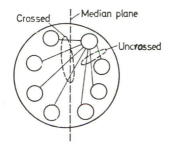

Figure 22
A simple explanation of crossed connections in the brain. When a median plane becomes defined in an animal with spherical symmetry, if each of the elements is connected to each of the others, there are more fibers crossing the median plane than fibers staying on one side. This little difference has been invoked as the ancestor of the much more imposing crossed connections in vertebrates.

jection may occur in invertebrate brains, it does not seem to be the general rule.

Possibly the best known explanation of the crossed representation of the world in the brain is that provided by Ramon y Cajal to account specifically for the crossing of the optic nerves, which he interpreted as a correction of the image inversion that occurs for reasons of geometrical optics in camera eyes (1). His argument is as follows. Suppose the right and left halves of the visual field are projected, with optical inversion, onto the right and left retinae. If these two half images were projected by uncrossed fiber bundles onto the right and left halves of a common receiving surface, there would be a midline discontinuity in the mapping of the visual field on this surface (figure 23A). Ramon y Cajal saw the chiasmal crossing as a simple means of avoiding this discontinuity (figure 23B).

The other sensory and motor systems, according to this theory, adapted secondarily to the crossed representation of the world in

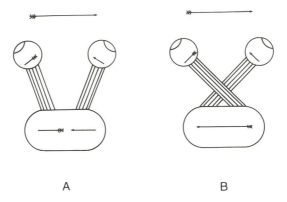

Figure 23
Ramon y Cajal's explanation of the crossed connections, starting from the inversion in the lens eye: the crossing reestablishes the continuity of the arrow B, which would otherwise be represented on the brain in the awkward fashion of A.

the brain. If visual images of objects to the right are being processed in the left brain, it is economical to let the motor commands for actions dealing with these objects (and presumably executed with the right extremities) also arise in the left hemisphere.

Several objections to Ramon y Cajal's argument may be raised, both on the basis of the reasoning involved and in the light of experimental results since his time.

1. Crossing is sufficient, but not necessary, for correction of optical inversion. For example, a 180° twist of uncrossed fiber bundles, or the equivalent internal crossing of fibers within each bundle, would permit correction without inversion of the image (figure 24:A,B). Similarly, recurved and uncrossed bundles projecting onto the posterior poles of the optic lobes would also correct for discontinuity (C).

2. The cogency of Cajal's argument presupposes an advantage in a continuous unbroken representation of the visual field in the

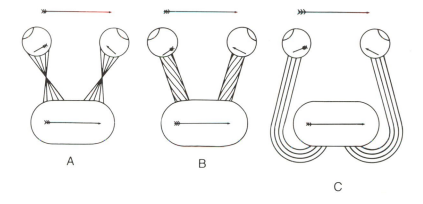

Figure 24
A weakness of Cajal's argument: crossing (A), or twisting (B) of individual bundles, or a detour to the back of the brain (C) would do the same trick.

brain. If the receiving surface is identified with the visual part of the midbrain, the so-called optic tectum—as Ramon y Cajal apparently did—then experimental studies of the topography of the projection on the tectum are pertinent. R. M. Gaze, for example, found in the frog an orderly projection of the left visual field onto the right tectum and vice versa (2). And the orientation of the two projections is indeed such that a continuous pattern in the visual field is represented again as a continuous pattern on the tectal surface, even if part of the pattern is seen by one eye and another part by the other eye. But it is difficult to see what use the optic tectum makes of this continuity, since there is no continuity of the gray substance across the midline. The two halves of the tectal nerve net are quite separate. It does not matter much how the two pieces are oriented to one other when the connection is made via fiber bundles of the white substance. Hence the optic tectum of the frog does not provide a good basis for an explanation of fiber crossing in terms of geometrical optics.

The compound eye of the fly: reconstruction of continuity in the visual representation (Vehicle 8)

I have myself given evidence for the correctness of the Cajal principle in another system of multiple fiber crossings found in the visual system of the fly. There the complicated weave of the fibers leading from the compound eye to the brain exactly compensates for the disruption of the image produced by each of the lenses projecting small inverted portions of the visual field onto the array of the light sensitive elements (3).

The compound eye of the fly is composed of about 3,000 nearly identical subunits, called ommatidia, each equipped with its own separate optics and containing 8 separate photosensitive elements, the rhabdomeres. Each rhabdomere is a specialized portion of one cell, the so-called retinula cell. The upper ends of 7 of these rhabdomeres in each ommatidium are arranged in a very regular pattern, localized in the focal plane of the inverting optical system. This pattern is called retinula (small retina) for a very good reason: to each rhabdomere corresponds a line of sight, and to the whole retinula 7 lines of sight, which intersect a distal plane in a pattern which is that of the retinula rotated by 180°.

The optical information discretely gathered by the elements of the retinula, and transformed by the visual pigments into the kinds of signals that are conveyed by nerve fibers, is carried down into the first visual ganglion—the lamina ganglionaris or simply lamina—through a bundle of 8 fibers emanating from the base of each ommatidium. It will come as no surprise that this nerve bundle is in fact twisted by 180°. The portion of the visual environment seen by each ommatidium has been inverted by the lens optics and could not fit continuously into the global picture provided by the noninverting array of ommatidia (an ommatidium pointing forward sees a portion of the environment situated in front of the animal, one pointing backward sees a posterior portion of the visual field, and so on) unless it were first re-rotated by 180° in the fiber bundle projecting to the ganglion (figures 25, 26).

There is even more precision to be discovered in this system: retinulae of neighboring ommatidia have their lines of sight so oriented that each is parallel, with great precision, to another line of sight in each of 6 neighboring ommatidia (4). This means that 7 retinula cells of 7 different ommatidia receive precisely the same visual information. (Here I simplify slightly, leaving out retinula cell number 8, which would complicate the issue but would not change the argument.) The law of the retina-to-lamina-projection is this: all the elements that look at the same point of the visual field send their axon into the same compartment of the ganglion (figure 26) (5).

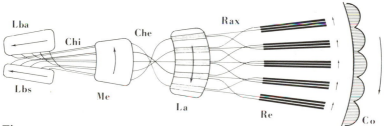

Figure 25

Diagram of the eye and visual ganglia of the fly. Co is the cornea, a set of lenses (in reality about 3,000). Re is the retina, with three light-sensitive elements ("rhabdomeres," in reality 7 for each lens) arranged with their tips in the focal planes of the lenses. Each lens projects an inverted image: the complicated weave of the axons below the retina, Rax, compensates for this and reconstructs the global picture on the first visual ganglion, La. There are further inversions of the picture in the outer chiasm (Che) and then again in the inner chiasm (Chi) between the second (Me) and the third (Lba, Lbs) visual ganglia, but these are not readily explained on functional grounds. Che is an example of an inversion that is not between the two halves of the brain but happens separately within each half.

The rigor with which this principle is carried through is especially astonishing in exceptional regions of the eye, such as near the margin (where an ommatidium has fewer neighbors than elsewhere) or near the "equator," where the arrangement of the retinula changes abruptly. Horridge and Meinertzhagen dedicated a very diligent study to the precision of this wiring and found absolutely no exceptions (6). It is easy to convince oneself that learning plays no part in the establishment of this type of connection because one finds the whole arrangement ready made in the late stages of pupation, long before the compound eye has ever received visual input (except for subdued and diffuse light, which may filter through the involucre of the pupa).

Olfactory orientation: control of behavior by symmetrical reins (Vehicles 1 to 4)

It is nice to see in the preceding example how a bit of physics, the geometrical optics of a lens, is incorporated precisely in a nerve net. But I have also argued that the lens in the vertebrate eye provides no convincing explanation for the crossed representation of the world in the brain (7). I proposed a different explanation, which takes as a starting point the one sense organ that has an uncrossed relation with the cerebral hemispheres, the sense of smell (figure 27). Each of the two olfactory tracts (the bundles of fibers carrying signals from the nose to the brain) goes straight to the cerebral hemisphere on the same side. The connections from the hemisphere to the motor system are crossed, however, which means that a certain smell has a stronger effect on the motor system on the side opposite the nostril it hits first or more strongly. This brings to mind schemes like those in Vehicles 2b and 3b, with all the properties we discussed there.

The most important nervous pathway in our primordial verte-

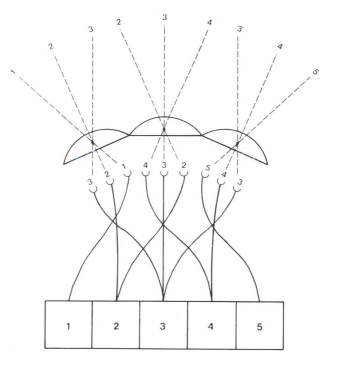

Figure 26
Explanation of the fiber pattern Rax between retina and brain. 123, 234, 345 are points in visual space seen by three adjoining lenses. Their projection is in the order 321, 432, 543. The fibers reestablish the original order 12345.

brate ancestors may well have been that between the nose and a set of muscles used for locomotion, since in the water the business of following chemical gradients is certainly important. The details, however, are not clear. First of all, we don't know what kinds of motors these primitive vertebrates used. If they were propelled primarily by a pair of fins, the case is analogous to that of our vehicles of type 2, in the sense that the thrust produced by the motor on one side of the animal (or vehicle) makes it turn toward

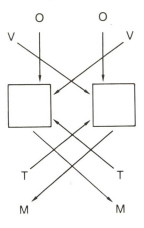

Figure 27
Crossing of visual (V) and tactile (T) input. Also the motor output is crossed (M). Only the olfactory input (O) is uncrossed.

the opposite side. The contrary is true for a fish, which relies mainly on a bending of its body for locomotion. In this case the contraction of the muscles on one side results in the animal turning to the same side. Also, it is not clear whether it is advantageous for a fish to turn toward the sources that activate its locomotion, a supposition I used to explain the crossing between the olfactory input and the motor output. Be this as it may, this sort of explanation of the crossed projection of the world in the brain may have its merits. It draws on a large body of observations on animal orientation and locomotion under the influence of various chemical and physical stimuli, with the older work well summarized in Fraenkel and Gunn (8). One of the originators of this tradition, Jacques Loeb, in a succession of books propagated a mechanistic approach quite similar to that of our vehicles (9). The outburst of zoological work in this field was largely prompted by negative reactions to his ideas.

Besides Vehicles 2 and 3, the very simple, so to speak, one-dimensional behavior of Vehicle 1 has biological counterparts in both the older literature and some recent work on bacteria (10).

Orientation and object fixation in flies (Vehicle 4)

Vehicle 4, with its nonlinear relation between sensory input and motor output, also brings to mind some neurophysiology. Such input-output characteristics are quite common at all levels. Movement of an object is not perceived visually if it is too slow or too fast and receives an optimal response at a certain angular velocity that is well known for flies and for men (11).

When the nonlinear relation of input-output is further complicated by varying characteristics of a set of detectors depending on their position in a sensory field, the ensuing behavior may become quite complicated. Or, the other way around, it is sometimes possible to explain astonishingly complex behavior, such as that of a fly navigating through a room and landing on a hanging lamp, by invoking nothing but a set of almost identical, rather simple movement detectors whose output, weighted for position, converges on a few motoneurons. This idea appears in some recent work by Reichardt (12) and has its precursor in early explanations of phototropism (13).

Consider again the compound eye of an insect. We have already seen that it is composed of a great number of almost identical units, each with its lens and associated sensory and neural apparatus. It is a fact that in many insects most of the information that enters the brain from the eye is not about where light and dark spots are in the visual field but about where something moves and in what direction, independent of what it is that moves. This is of course important information when an insect wants to control its own position in its visual environment during flight. Rotation of all points of the visual field around a certain axis most likely signifies simply that the animal has itself been turning (in the opposite direction) around that axis.

Forward movement of a flying fly produces a more complicated visual flow field: the panorama streams through the visual field in a backward direction, with the flowing motion seemingly emanating from the point of forward projection of the direction of flight. But the velocity of the flow depends on several factors, including the angle the line of sight forms with the direction of motion of the animal and the distance from the eye of the various objects forming the visual environment. The measurement of the velocity vectors in every part of the visual field of a flying insect obviously provides a great deal of information, but we are hard put when we try to invent schemes that would extract the relevant information for the life of the insect, and make use of it.

Once again, it may be simpler than it looks: another instance of the law of uphill analysis and downhill synthesis. One of the observations about flying flies was their tendency to navigate toward isolated objects on a homogeneous background. They do this in very complicated experiments by Reichardt. And they also do it in real life when they settle on a branch or on somebody's nose. A simple explanation is this (figure 28). Generally, perceived motion in the visual field makes the fly turn in the direction of the motion. The effect of the perceived motion may be different for different directions, however. Say, motion of an object in the backward direction in the right half field makes the fly turn toward the right more vigorously than the forward motion of the same object in the same position makes the fly turn toward the left. Try to imagine what happens if that object wiggles (or if the fly's head vibrates, which has the same effect). With every wiggle toward the back the fly turns toward the object a little more than it turns away from it with the wiggle in the opposite direction. In the end the fly will be facing the object.

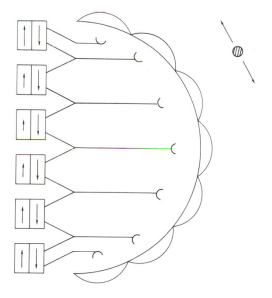

Figure 28

The turning tendency induced by movement in two opposite directions may not be of the same magnitude (represented by the different lengths and directions of the arrows). This will produce a tendency to turn toward wiggling objects on a stationary or void background. The difference between the forward and backward reaction may vary according to position in the eye (arrows).

In reality things are slightly more complicated but still of the same nature. It seems that the difference between the effects of forward and backward motion varies in a systematic way over the visual field. Thus for every pattern in the visual field there will be a net turning tendency, compounded out of the many contributions of turning tendency from each point of the visual field. The complicated trajectory of a fly in your room may be, in a way, a peculiar sort of image of that room, the velocity and the maneuvers of the fly being completely determined by the initial velocity of the fly and by the distribution of visual detail in the environment.

Another well-known instance of nonlinear input-output relations is apparent in the reactions of many animals to the sight of other animals or moving objects. This depends in a curious manner on the size of the other animal (or object): small specimens elicit prey-catching behavior, very large ones elicit flight, and intermediate-size objects are examined in more detail. Something of this sort has been shown even at the level of electrophysiological studies of single neurons in the visual system of the toad (14).

McCulloch–Pitts neurons and real neurons (Vehicle 5)

Vehicle 5 is, of course, an embodiment of the old McCulloch and Pitts "Logical calculus of the ideas immanent in nervous activity" (15). This was one of the great boosters of modern brain science. Its experimental basis is in electrophysiological studies on the spinal cord.* The influence of one input nerve ("posterior root") of the spinal cord on one output nerve ("anterior root") is under certain conditions "monosynaptic": the fibers of the posterior root directly contact the motoneurons from which the fibers of the anterior root originate.

---

*A glossary may be helpful for readers who are not trained in the biological sciences. *Neuron:* a special kind of cell devoted to signal transmission in the nervous system. *Dendrites:* usually ramified appendages of the neuron, which carry signals toward the central part of the neuron. *Axon:* a single usually ramified appendage of the neuron which carries signals away from the center of the neuron. *Nerve:* a bundle of axons. *Synapse:* the place where the axon of one neuron transmits signals to a dendrite (or cell body) of another. *Motoneuron:* a neuron of the central nervous system connected to a muscle. *Sensory neuron:* a neuron directly connected to, and influenced by, a sense organ.

When the cooperation of various input nerves in the activation of spinal motoneurons was analysed, three facts emerged. They turned out to be fundamental discoveries about the computational properties of synapses, even before the techniques of electrical recording of single neurons were developed (16). For some of the motoneurons, the conjoined activity of several inputs is necessary in order to activate them. In other cases the fibers of one input nerve are by themselves sufficient to reach the thresholds of the neurons. And finally, a third kind of situation seemed to imply that some fibers inhibit the motoneurons, in the sense that their activation from other sources is made ineffective. These inferences from macroscopical input-output experiments were later confirmed with microelectrode studies; they were explained as consequences of the electrical properties of the neural cell membrane and of the influence of chemical transmitter substances on these properties (17).

In their famous paper McCulloch and Pitts stylized the functional relations of neurons connected by synapses as the fundamental operations of the calculus of propositions: conjunction, disjunction, and negation (*and, or,* and *not*). These are fundamental in the sense that they were the first logical relations to be used for that purpose in antiquity by the Greek philosophers. But they are not unique; many other sets of such fundamental relations would do, or even one single relation (there are two relations with this property: *not both,* and *both not*), which could of course be called fundamental with much more right.

Is it an accident, then, that conjunction, disjunction, and negation were first defined by the philosophers and then rediscovered as fundamental properties of neurons and synapses in the spinal cord? Or is the nervous system really constructed out of these operations, with the consequence that the philosophers can only discover in their own thinking the laws that make their brains tick? Or did Sherrington describe the phenomena of facilitation, occlusion, and inhibition in terms that were subconsciously suggested to him by the philosophical teachings to which he was subjected in his schools and perhaps implicitly through ideas incorporated in the English language? I have no answer.

The McCulloch–Pitts theory of nerve nets is one of the roots of the theory of automata (18), so much so that in the early years some people who really had computing machinery in mind used the words "neuron" and "synapse" and drew diagrams that were originally intended to depict real nerve nets in animal brains (19).

It was indeed practical to speak of neurons and of threshold devices synonymously, but there are good reasons why I preferred the latter terms in the description of the vehicles' brains. Real neurons have properties that go far beyond the simple threshold devices we used as building blocks for our vehicles' brains. True, the most important signal by which patterns of activity are represented within animal brains is the "action potential," an explosive event that happens in its entirety or does not happen at all and, when it happens, is propagated with undiminished intensity along the fibers leading to other neurons. This obviously implies the concept of threshold because a certain minimal intensity of excitation is required to set off the explosive event. But it is debatable whether these thresholds play the role that we assign them when we think of logical computation by means of threshold devices. First of all, it is difficult to imagine such computation without a clock that keeps strict order in time. In the McCulloch–Pitts theory, as in digital computers, the temporal coordinate is represented by a sequence of discrete instants, with all the changes in the activity of the network happening between one instant and the next.

In real brains this is hardly so. The exact point in time at which an action potential arises in a neuron depends not only on the time at which the excitation reaches the neuron but also on the intensity of excitation (figure 29). Just as the potential across a condensor reaches a certain value faster the stronger the current that charges the condensor, the critical level of the potential across the nerve cell

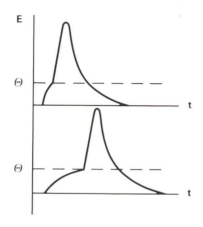

Figure 29
Dependence of the action potential on the intensity of stimulation. The shape of the rapid excursion of the potential E (above the dashed line) does not change with different intensities of stimulation, while the charging time required to meet the threshold is shorter for higher intensity stimulation (upper curve).

membrane (which triggers the spike) is also reached more quickly when the excitation is strong. Thus the amount of excitation above the threshold is lost in the ordinary threshold element of a computing device but not in the brain where it translates into the time of occurrence of the action potential. A consequence of this is the desynchronization of action potentials triggered by synchronous excitation in a block of nerve tissue. Whether two spikes will meet or not at a certain synaptic junction, and hence whether the logical operation performed by that junction will occur, may depend on just these unwanted delays (figure 30). The simple interpretation of a nerve net as an automaton with a fixed structure, operating synchronously on a discrete time scale, therefore becomes less likely.

This is not to say that neurons may not occasionally trigger all-or-nothing reactions. Very quick actions, such as occur in situations of danger or in reaction-time experiments in a psychological laboratory, or in sports, must be governed by sequences of very few action potentials in the neurons of the motor system. With neurons producing action potentials at a frequency of the order of 10 or 100 per second, the reaction to a stimulus that occurs in less than 0.1 seconds must be triggered by the first, or by the first few action potentials.

However, in many other situations, well studied by neurophysiologists, the signal within the brain corresponding to a sensory stimulus is a burst of action potentials rather than a single action potential. In such bursts, very commonly the frequency varies with

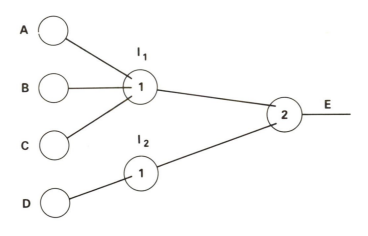

Figure 30
The effect described in figure 29 applied to a small nerve net. In this figure either A, B, or C alone, or two or three of them in combination, activate the interneuron I_1 which has a threshold equal to one unit of excitation. But the more input elements that are active, the sooner interneuron I_1 will produce its potential. Thus when A, B, C, and D are active at the same time, coincidence of the output of I_1 and I_2 at E may not occur any more. This is to show that threshold elements on a discrete time scale may not be an accurate description of neurons.

the intensity of the stimulus. Borrowing terms from computer engineering: there is an analogue principle involved in this which is quite foreign to the digital operation of the McCulloch–Pitts nerve net, or to the automation of automata theory. We are far from understanding the code or, what is more likely, the different kinds of codes that are used between nerve cells in the brain. One point of information theory, however, remains valid: all messages can be represented in theory by discrete signals on a limited number of elements. This is the reason why the vehicles' brains, made out of threshold devices very different from live neurons, may still display some very lifelike properties of information handling.

Most readers will have recognized the vehicle leaving marks on the beach as a very elementary version of a Turing machine. For those who are not familiar with this concept, I recommend either Turing's original articles or Minsky's book of 1967, or the very friendly introduction in J. Sampson (20).

The very last sentence on Vehicle 5 must by necessity remain cryptic, because the idea is not yet fully worked out. What I refer to is the increase in computing power of a brain that is endowed with the power of learning. No doubt this makes it possible for the brain to write down its own record in the pattern of its interneuronal connections, and then read it off again. But the way this is done is very different from the way a Turing machine works with its tape, printing, and reading heads.

Evolution (Vehicle 6)

The game we are playing to generate the vehicles of type 6 hushes up most of the complexity of Darwinian evolution. My aim was not to make propaganda for this theory. It is all too obviously correct for the people who are enchanted by its power of demystification, while others will forever invent difficulties and counterarguments. *The Selfish Gene* by Dawkins (21) is a book on evolution that should appeal to psychologists. It is not weighted down by an obscure desire that biology should not arise from physics after all. Of course there are the classics of evolutionary theory (22). Prepared by Dawkins, even the reader with no interest in biology will enjoy the information-generating capacity of the evolutionary process in an adventure in psychology.

Memory (Vehicles 7, 10, 11, 12, 13, 14)

Beginning with Vehicle 7, we considered a property of nerve tissue unmatched by anything in present-day technology, the distributed memory acting on the logical structure of the network itself. In nearly all technical realizations, including electronic simulations of nerve nets, information that goes into the memory is deposited separately, outside of the computing machinery, often in equipment that is entirely different from that doing the computing. This is because neither Mnemotrix nor Ergotrix wire are commercially available. Indeed, if an engineer reads about our vehicles, I am sure he will be irritated by the glib way in which I have assumed the feasibility of something which to him would appear as the main technical problem to be solved.* However, I am not alone. Uttley's "conditional probability machine" assumes elements with properties similar to a piece of Ergotrix wire (23), and Steinbuch's "Lernmatrix" does not work without Mnemotrix junctions (24).

These models and many others, notably the very influential (verbally formulated) model by D. O. Hebb (25), were all created under the impression that "association" is the most important principle by which information about the environment is incorporated into

---

*Professor Stefano Crespi Reghizzi in Milan did read the manuscript and was irritated. I thank him cordially for his comments.

the brain. When things occur together, the neurons that signal their occurrence will also be somehow connected in the brain. Is this assumption correct? Richard Sutton and Andrew Barto (26) argue that it is perhaps too simple an assumption, in view of emerging information about the complexity of the operation of individual neurons. And they argue that association may not be sufficient to produce the effects that must be explained in cognitive psychology. We have already discussed (in Vehicles 13 and 14) the aspect of prediction, which these authors stress.

At this point we ask instead whether there is any direct physiological evidence, based on microelectrode studies on single neurons, which makes the phenomenon of association more concrete, evidence beyond the almost inescapable but indirect assumption derived from psychology. The answer, since Hubel and Wiesel (27) is yes, there is such evidence, at least of this form: artificially induced squint in kittens, which disrupts the normal cooperation between the two eyes, has the effect that some of the normal connections between the eyes and the cortical nerve cells will not be formed. Apparently, the pattern of these connections is molded by experience.

The principle that can best explain these observations is the following (figure 31). A cortical nerve cell that is at first diffusely but weakly connected to a large number of input fibers from both eyes, with time and experience picks those fibers from the right and the left eye that mostly carry the same signals. The cortical nerve cell then makes strong connection with them at the expense of the other input fibers. This way it is assured that individual nerve cells of the visual cortex receive signals from corresponding portions of the two retinas and hence from the same point in the visual field. The principle of association is apparent in this: related activity leads to the making of a connection. At a more macroscopic level the physiology of association was established before the introduction of the microelectrode (28). The pairing of electrical stimuli to different

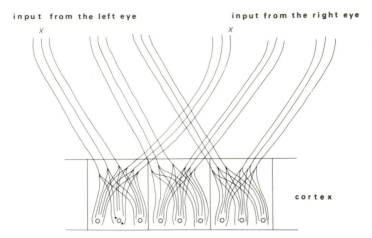

Figure 31

Refinement of the projection of visual input onto the visual cortex by a learning process. Fibers from both eyes reach the cortex in a rough topographical order, such that bundles of fibers from corresponding places of the two eyes are intermingled in the same compartment of the cortex. Subsequently individual cortical neurons pick fibers from both eyes which are mostly active at the same time (X) and make strong connections with them (dots). Thus cortical neurons become connected to retinal elements having exactly the same coordinates in the right and left eyes.

parts of the brain had the consequence that one of the two loci yielded behavioral effects of stimulation previously associated only with the other locus.

In search of an engram: the anatomy of memory (Vehicles 7, 11)

In a way these results are quite obvious and could be expected. Granted that signals are carried by fibers and synapses from the sense organs through the brain to the muscles, how would we explain that a few neurons in the acoustic centers of a rat's brain, responding to the sound of a buzzer, at first have no influence on the motoneurons of the rat's forepaw but after some training regularly lead to movement there, if not by supposing some anatomical rerouting, that is, changes in the synapses of the network? It is an entirely different matter if we ask what exactly has happened in the tissue, and at what level. There are still people who think that the growth of new dendrites is involved, or the degeneration of already existing ones, while others prefer to think in terms of axonal growth or degeneration. It is fashionable now to say that the changes probably take place in already existing individual synapses that are ready to learn. But this hardly explains the changes in the size of the brain, which some claim are associated with the acquisition of information: the more information is acquired by the brain, they say, the bigger the brain becomes (29). In fact the synapses occupy only a tiny fraction of the volume of the brain.

It is no longer fashionable, luckily, to imagine that the information of complex experiences resides in individual molecules of the brain. There is of course plenty of ribonucleic acid in the cell bodies of nerve cells, and it is not quite clear what it does there. But this is not a good reason for supposing that its large information storage capacity, normally devoted to genetic information, in the brain codes happenings of the individual's life. This idea is actually irritating since the additional mechanisms it implicitly requires are more complicated than the facts it intends to explain. How is the information about the face, the name, and the utterances of somebody whom I just met distilled down to the minuscule codeword that fits into one molecule of one cell (which one?) in my brain? And worse still, how is the macroscopic pattern of action potentials in nerve cells that signals my meeting that person again compared to the minuscule trace left earlier so that I may be able to recognize him? Will it end up in the same cell in a parallel strand of ribonucleic acid? And how do I get the information out of the molecule when I want to describe that person?

The experimental approaches to the question of the anatomical nature of the engram are all marred by a fundamental difficulty. (Engrams are the memory traces postulated many years ago by psychologists, long before there was any hope of ever finding one in the brain.) Suppose we have some idea about the anatomical changes responsible for memory and want to prove it. We present some input to one animal, but not to another animal, in order to use it as a control. It is not that the control animal has experienced nothing while the experimental animal received its input: it has had its own experiences and its own thoughts. In order to compare the traces left in the brains of the two animals by the two different inputs, we would have to know exactly where the information ended up in the two animals. In truth we don't. Most likely, two inputs that may have entirely different meanings are represented in the brain in quite the same way, as diffuse patterns of activity in an enormous network of neurons.

Suppose the engram were embodied in changes that are very easily visible in the electron microscope, or possibly in the light microscope: a change in the thickness of axonal terminals, a change in the number of synaptic vesicles, or a change in the amount of pre- or postsynaptic thickening. No matter what kind of information we presented to the animal, in the end we would expect to see some synapses of one kind and some of the other, for information must be represented in a pattern of elements in different states, or else it wouldn't be information at all. But different patterns can only be distinguished if they are understood in every detail. In other words, they cannot be distinguished at the present stage of our knowledge of the brain.

There is of course the possibility of imposing input of a brutally abnormal kind, by keeping an animal entirely in the dark or by keeping one of its eyes blinded. In these cases, which are called deprivation experiments, anatomical changes can indeed be found in the brain, but it remains questionable whether they are of the same kind as the changes underlying memory in the normal upbringing of an animal. It would not be surprising if the development of the brain just does not happen in the normal way in a mouse that never sees the light of day, perhaps for reasons connected with an abnormal condition of the hormonal system rather than lack of sensory information.

There are some animals, however, in which the deprivation experiment, so to speak, is a part of normal development, and the controls are also furnished by nature. What I have in mind is the comparison of brains in related species, such as rabbit and hare, rat and guinea pig—of which one is born very immature and the other is born at a much later stage in its embryonic development. Rats are born tiny, naked, blind, helpless creatures, while guinea pigs resemble the adult animal in their appearance and their behavior immediately after birth. If the development of the brain is studied in the two species from early stages on (30), it appears that there are no great differences, except that the exit from the uterus happens at a later date on the developmental calendar in one case than it does in the other.

There are some stages in the development of the rat brain that happen after birth and can be influenced by environmental stimuli: this finding was sometimes hailed as a paradigm of the anatomy of learning. The same episode in the development of the guinea pig brain takes place when the fetus is entirely (or almost entirely) shielded from environmental influences in the maternal womb. Thus the structures that develop at that time (for example, the dendrites and axons of cortical neurons, dendritic spines, most synapses) at least in the guinea pig and presumably also in the normal rat do not encode messages from the environment.

We have to take a closer look (31): the anatomical changes that subserve memory must be finer than that. Schüz presents some good candidates, subtle differences between the biologically mature but psychologically inexperienced brains of newborn guinea pigs and the brains of adult experienced animals: differences in the shape of synapses on electron micrographs and differences in the number of synaptic vesicles, as well as quite macroscopic differences in the shape of the "dendritic spines," which carry most of the synapses in the cerebral cortex. What makes these changes good candidates for memory traces is that the variance increases with age. We would be disappointed if some change in the structure of synapses affected all synapses of the cerebral cortex in the same way. We would then call it an effect of aging rather than of learning, since memory traces ought to differentiate between neurons to be effective.

Maps and their use (Vehicles 8, 9)

It is all too obvious that Vehicles 8 and 9 have not sprung merely from creative fancy. They incorporate the one aspect of animal brains that has been the main theme of brain research for the past hundred years: the representation of external spaces in the spatial coordinates of the nervous system. We used to think in the past that such maps of the world (or of the body surface) in the brain were a prerogative of the primary sensory and motor fields, for example, in the cerebral cortex. But recently more refined techniques have revealed a succession of visual, tactile, auditory, and motor maps, covering most of the available space in the brain (32).

One wonders where the sort of computation that is not related in any obvious way to geometrical space takes place. Intuitively, we have no use for 2- or 3-dimensional Cartesian coordinates in the context of language or in the abstract world of concepts related by a multitude of associative connections, nowadays often described under the heading "semantic nets" (33). Intuition may of course be misleading in this field, as we are told by Lieblich and Arbib (34) and also by some of the discussants of their paper, who point out that simple cartography cannot be the whole story even in portions of the cerebral cortex that are clearly related, point by point, to some sensory space. Maps are meaningless, they warn us, unless we have a process for using them. The concept of the world graph, which they propose, makes the distinction less drastic between information handling in geometrically defined spaces and information handling in the abstract spaces of language and the like.

There is no doubt in my mind about the functional importance of these orderly representations, quite in the spirit of the tricks described in Vehicle 8, although in theory other explanations are possible on embryological grounds. If the problem is to connect a million sense cells to a million cells in the brain, one of the simplest solutions is of course to let a whole bundle of fibers find its way, instead of specifying the address for each individual fiber. The preserved order in the projection may just be due to the preserved neighborhood relations of the fibers in the bundle, and it would be idle then to speculate about the functional meaning of the resulting "map."

This cannot be the whole story, however. The tricks requiring an internal representation of neighborhood, which we introduced in Vehicles 8 and 9, have clearly been inspired by functional principles known to operate in animal brains. A great deal is known about the characteristics of movement detectors in the visual systems of various animals, including flies, as we have already seen. Cells that respond to moving stimuli have been identified in the retina of the rabbit (35). In a beetle (Chlorophanus) the properties and the arrangement of a set of visual movement detectors were defined in a quantitative way by Hassenstein, Reichardt, and Varju (36), although the corresponding histology could not be identified with certainty. In the fly (37), much more is known now about the various levels of integration in the visual ganglia, including some neuroanatomy revealing fiber patterns of such stupendous precision that they seem to be taken out of some mechanical vehicle's brain (38).

Lateral inhibition also has solid experimental foundations. Since it was discovered in human visual (39), auditory, and tactile (40) perception, it was also described as a principle of neuronal interaction in the eye of the horseshoe crab Limulus Polyphemus (41) and after that in all too many other situations. Its simplicity and powerful information-handling properties invited mathematical formalization (42) and various speculations on its role as a basic computational device in central nerve nets, such as the cerebellum (43) and the cerebral cortex (44).

A word about the idea that led to the construction of figure 15: networks may be symmetric in any number of dimensions and still be housed comfortably in the 3-dimensional space surrounding us, or even in the 2-dimensional space of a drawing. This was just intended as a warning to neuroanatomists who cannot abstract from what they see. It is conceivable that the exact analysis of a piece of nerve tissue may reveal a connectivity not at all apparent in the external shape, for instance a truly 4-dimensional network compressed into an ordinary 3-dimensional body. But I know of no such case.

What happens is that occasionally a sensory manifold of more than two dimensions is projected onto the usual kind of cortex-like nerve net which, for all we know, is essentially 2-dimensional. There is a well-known example in vision. Although each eye receives a two-dimensional picture of the visual environment, the combination of the two pictures provides information about three-dimensional visual space. And indeed, the two pictures are brought together in one and the same piece of cortex, the visual cortex, where this information is presumably extracted. But before 3-dimensional space is reconstructed, the two pictures are projected onto the cortical surface in a peculiar way, with narrow stripes of the picture from one eye alternating with stripes from the other eye, all on the same plane, sharing the same 2-dimensional coordinates of the cortex (45). We still don't know how the third dimension of space, which is lost in the projection, is later regained through stereoscopic vision and where it is represented in the brain, but it seems almost certain that its representation is not orthogonal to that of the other two dimensions, that is, to the plane of the visual cortex.

One saving thought: if the detection of continuous trajectories is one of the points of the orderly representation of sensory spaces, the loss of one dimension in the projection does not matter much, since a continuous trajectory in the original space always has as its image a continuous line in the projection, and a discontinuous line has a discontinuous projection most of the time.

Shapes. The morphemes of visual perception (Vehicle 9)

Vehicle 9 is especially dedicated to the memory of Gestalt psychology. Under this denomination, which means nothing but the study of the concept of shape, a group of brilliant psychologists during the first third of this century set out to discover the laws that make similar shapes look similar to humans (46). How right they were in making an issue out of this problem became clear to everybody, including computer engineers, when, much later, they tried to construct efficient machines for the discrimination of forms (47) (enemy airplanes, handwritten addresses, turbulent or nonturbulent cloud patterns).

Gestalt psychologists were not so successful, however, in their attempts at relating their discoveries to functional principles of brain physiology. Not enough was known at the time about the neurons and their connections in the brain, and what was known was often presented in a form that tended to obscure the computer-like aspects. Today much more is known about the brain, but progress is slow in this field and we still have to rely mostly on speculation (48). We are just beginning to grasp some of the codewords the brain uses in categorizing shapes, the elements of meaning that we project into our visual environment or, to use a term from linguistics, the morphemes of visual perception. Here are some examples.

Clustering is undoubtedly the most fundamental element of form perception, the most obvious morpheme in the brain. The Pleiades are perceived as a unitary object in the sky because of the rather uniform brightness of a number of stars clustering in that region. And indeed, the morpheme "local density" in this case corresponds to a physical reality, the gravitational coupling and common origin of these stars. Another example: a number of sounds, all rich in high frequency components, indicate the presence of an animal moving nearby in the underbrush. The neuronal activity clustering in the region of the acoustic system where high frequencies are represented is immediately discovered by other neurons, which relay signals to an alerting system in the brain.

Clustering of neuronal activity may be a factor even after several stages of abstraction from the sense data, as when we immediately perceive movement of disparate objects in widely separated parts of the visual field when their movement is in the same direction and at the same velocity. This is the "common fate" phenomenon of Gestalt psychology, recently reproposed as a puzzle in neurophysiology by H. B. Barlow (49). Here the clustering is not in a region of the brain where visual space is mapped but perhaps in another region where we may suppose an orderly representation of velocities occurs.

The detection of clusters has a clear counterpart in neuroanatomy. The neurons in the brain are highly branched, star-shaped objects whose size in many cases, notably in the cerebral cortex, is larger by at least a factor of 10 than the separation of their centers. Their dendritic trees are fairly uniformly covered with synapses, several thousands for each neuron, through which they receive their input. (They are also connected to each other.) Thus each responds to the activation of a cloud of synapses centered around it, and the clouds of synapses belonging to neighboring neurons overlap generously. Some dendritic trees of smaller neurons are even fully contained within the dendritic spread of larger neurons (figure 32). We

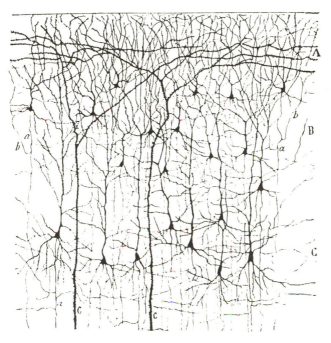

Figure 32
From Cajal, 1911. Golgi picture of the upper layers of the human visual cortex. Only a small percentage of the total neuronal population is shown, all of them of the pyramidal kind. The size of their dendritic ramification varies a great deal. Only part of the apical dendrites are shown for some enormous neurons of the lower layers, the spread of which greatly exceeds that of the other neurons in the picture (ascending dendrites marked c).

realize how we are able to see densities of dots using neurons with large dendritic spread at the same time as we resolve individual dots, and even the contours of individual dots, using the smaller neurons of the same region in the visual cortex.

There is even something like a neuronal "zoom" embodied in this structure. Figure 33 gives rise to the following observation. In the reproduction of part of an eighteenth-century etching above, the smoothness and curvature of the skin is admirably rendered by

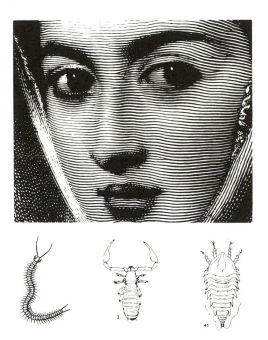

Figure 33

The neuronal zoom effect. We integrate visually over the hatching, which admirably renders the smooth skin in the engraving above. But shifting our glance to the animals below, we are ready immediately to count the legs of the centipede or to describe the shape of the book scorpion's claws, details far finer than the spacing of the lines of the hatching.

variations in the density of quasi-parallel black and white lines. Individual lines are seen only if attention is drawn especially to them. On the contrary, if we glance at the legs of the centipede below, the segments of the bodies of the three arthropods, or the shape of the claws of the book scorpion, all their structural details are immediately recognized as such with the full spatial resolution our eyes afford. Note that the periodicity of the centipede is narrower than that of the hatching above and the small numbers next to the zoological illustrations are no larger than the spacing of the lines of the shading.

This observation implies that we are able to switch rapidly from one set of filters to another, making available to the form-perceiving mechanism different bands of the space-frequency spectrum. In terms of the neurons in the cortex (figure 32), it seems that sets of smaller and larger neurons (by a factor of at least 5) can take over in the coding of the visual input, depending on which set of neurons provides the picture that makes the most sense to the brain.

Another category of visual perception is the continuity of lines and of trajectories. Like clustering, it is implicitly embodied in the structure of nerve nets as we see them under a microscope; it also provides good evidence for the usefulness of internal maps. It certainly is not difficult to invent a network of "neurons" with connections between neighbors (figure 34) providing facilitation such that the input becomes effective only if one of the neighboring elements has received input a moment earlier. Such a network would give a much stronger response for a patch of excitation moving smoothly over its surface than for disjoint patches or discontinuous movement. This is a common type of connectivity (for example, in the system of axon collaterals in the cerebral cortex), although for some reason the facilitating connections between neighbors seem to be less easily detected in the electrophysiological experiments than the inhibitory ones.

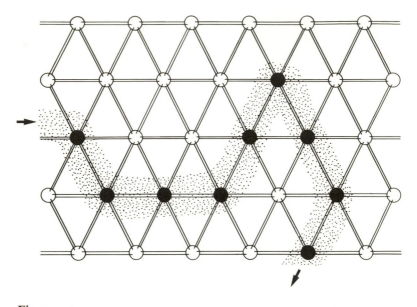

Figure 34

A network that responds to continuous trajectories. Neighboring elements excite each other subliminally. They can be fully excited by the input (black dots) only if a neighbor was excited a moment before. Thus only continuous trajectories (for example the one indicated by the stippling) are perceived.

It is clear that a network such as the one in figure 34 can provide the most convincing clues for the distinction between real objects and random noise or hallucinations, for the most common thing that can be said about physical objects is that they move at reasonable speeds without breaks in their trajectories. The disturbing thing is that, at least in visual perception, the continuity of a line is not necessarily detected at this trivial level. Kanizsa (50) has given examples in which lines can be seen that are not at all contained in the pattern presented (figure 35). They are apparently constructed,

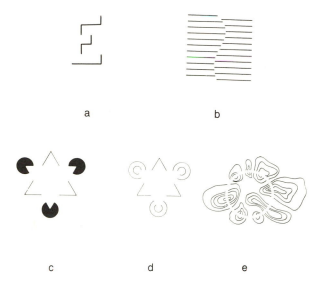

Figure 35

Contours that are not present in the picture are reconstructed through an active process of interpretation. a: from Brunswik, 1935; b: from Kennedy, 1974; c, d, and e: from Kanisza, 1974, all quoted in Metzger, 1975.

in much the same way for every observer, by some active process that may have its roots partly in experience and partly in inborn mechanisms. We learn from this that it is somewhat artificial and unnecessary to draw a sharp line between perceptual and cognitive processes (51).

It would be surprising if it turned out that the visual category of bilateral symmetry is not related to the symmetrical build of the two halves of the brain and to their point-to-point connections in the simple way I suggested in Vehicle 9. This very strong element of form, mirror symmetry with respect to a vertical line situated in front of the animal (52), has an obvious counterpart in neuro-anatomy: the commissures connecting symmetrical points of the right and left brain. The most imposing commissure, the corpus callosum, contains about 200 million fibers in man, about one hundred times more than the fibers in the two optic nerves. By an argument of sheer information capacity, this system of fibers must do more than simply compare the visual input in the two halves of the visual field, which are projected onto the two halves of the brain. No doubt bilateral symmetry is also an important property in other sensory or motor contexts. Actually, the primary visual area is one of the exceptions in the general scheme of callosal connections: it contributes very few fibers to the corpus callosum, but the secondary and tertiary visual areas, where the higher-order figure analysis is sometimes supposed to take place, are abundantly connected by fibers between symmetrical points in the right and left brain.

In some cases even the wildest speculations do not lead to satisfactory explanations. One good thing about computer technology is the possibility of immediately translating speculations into machines. Their worth is thereby quickly revealed and the turnover of ideas is increased. We can no longer fondle our ideas about the brain with the secure feeling that their falsification is beyond technical feasibility. Most ideas can be translated into computer programs and are thus easily put to the experimental test.

And yet many aspects of perception are still a mystery. Nobody knows by what principle we are able to recognize without fail individual human faces out of millions. Even if we reduce the problem to that of the recognition of profiles, we notice that the perception and distinction of contours has by no means been fully understood. Contours are extracted out of the original visual input most likely by the process of lateral inhibition, which is familiar to us from the discussion of Vehicle 8 (figure 14). No doubt they carry most of the information we need in dealing with the objects of our environment, as we all know from the use of drawings as the most

Figure 36
Various kinds of arrowheads. Their essence is described by the abstract figure on the right.

widespread means of nonverbal communication (at least before the introduction of photographs).

But how contours are further analyzed in the brain is not at all clear, except for one thing: it probably is not done the way computer engineers do it, judging from the meager success of their attempts to replace human observers with machines in crucial situations. I think what we humans do in the perception of contours must embody at least the two principles illustrated in figures 36 and 37. For one thing, we categorize shapes roughly by the presence or absence of appendages, which may interfere with our motor acts when we deal with an object of that shape, and by the relative position of those appendages. For instance, the dangerous function of a barbed arrowhead is fully described by the abstract scheme that we call an arrowhead in technical graphics and is quite independent of the details of the contour (figure 36). On the other hand, we take in a surprising amount of information about minute variations of curvature. We are able to detect immediately the discontinuity in the second derivative of curves that are composed of four arcs of circles, while something in our perception (the "inner eye"?—the gaze does no such thing) glides pleasantly along the smoothly changing curvature of the one true ellipse (figure 37).

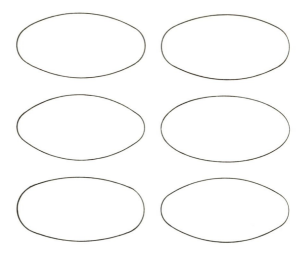

Which is the ellipse?

Figure 37
Detection of discontinuities in the second derivative. Five of these curves are composed of arcs of circles of different radii. Only one corresponds to a single algebraic expression of second degree. It is easily identified by everyone (from Scheffers, 1911) (53).

It is tempting to think of Hubel and Wiesel's line segment detectors in the visual cortex as the elements of a differential analysis of curves in visual space (54). We are told that in any small region of the cortex about half a millimeter across there are representatives of all orientations in the set of line segment detectors, and there are some that see white lines and others that see black lines or even dividing lines between white and black. Since half a millimeter cortex in the central part of the visual field corresponds to little more than the unit of resolution of the visual system, we get the impression that besides location and color, orientation is another dimension in which the visual input is coded at the elementary level.

But we know very little about the possible mechanisms of interaction between the neighboring line segment detectors we must postulate in order to explain our proficiency in the detection not only of curvature but also of changes of curvature (figure 37). The feature detectors of Hubel and Wiesel up to now explain only first, not second and third derivatives.

An inborn category of acoustic form perception (Vehicles 8, 9)

In acoustics some of the inborn categories of perception are well documented in their relation to physiological facts. To most of us a melody played in different keys remains practically identical to itself. This very astonishing fact is well explained by the finding that in the cortex of the brain, as on a piano keyboard, frequencies are represented on a logarithmic scale (figure 38) (55). The resulting translational symmetry for tone patterns characterized by constant frequency ratios is one of the basic facts of music. It may reflect our ability to roughly recognize the shape of a solid body by the acoustic frequencies it emits when it is mechanically solicited. This pattern is independent of the size of the object when it is defined in terms of frequency ratios.

Structure of the cerebral cortex (Vehicle 11)

We are getting to our more cognitive vehicles, numbers 10 to 14. From here on it becomes increasingly difficult to provide direct justification for the vehicles by pointing out experimental facts about animal brains. Rather, the connection is with both kinds of psychology: serious academic psychology about animal

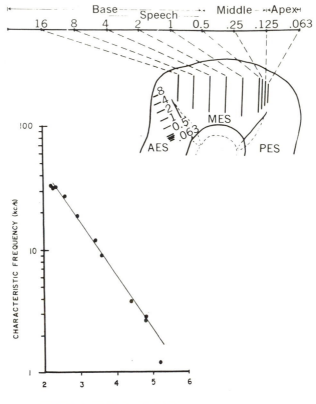

Figure 38

An a priori of music: the logarithmic plot of acoustic frequencies in the brain. Above (from Tunturi, 1962): projection of the frequency scale (numbers stand for kilohertz) on the middle ectosylvian gyrus (MES) and again on the anterior ectosylvian gyrus (AES) of the dog cortex. Both projections are linear on a logarithmic scale between about 250 and 8,000 (16,000) hertz. Doubling of the frequency corresponds to equal distances on the cortex. Only for very low frequencies this relation breaks down. Below (from Evans, 1968): a similar plot in the ventral cochlear nucleus of the cat. Logarithm of frequency versus position in the nucleus is linear (55).

learning and behavior on the one hand, and the introspective psychology of thinking (of which we are all specialists) on the other.

However, the distinction between two kinds of association, which is introduced in Vehicle 11, is not only appealing on philosophical grounds but may find an interpretation in terms of neuroanatomy. To make this plausible, I will provide an introduction to the cerebral cortex by quoting from some of my recent papers (56).

According to somewhat divergent estimates, the number of nerve cells in both hemispheres of the cerebral cortex of man amounts to about 10 billion. The majority of these belong to a type called the pyramidal cell. It is characterized, among other things, by an axon leaving the cortex at one point in order to reenter it at another and to make synaptic connections there. Compared to the 10^{10} internal connections of the cortex, the number of afferent fibers entering the cortex from regions outside the cortex seems relatively small. The fibers bringing information from all the senses together do not exceed the order of magnitude 10^6, of which the largest number belongs to visual input. It is difficult to estimate the magnitude of fiber bundles reaching the cortex from other parts of the brain, although the number of cells in the thalamus, from which the greatest part of this so-called nonspecific input to the cortex originates, may serve as an upper limit. It does not exceed the order of 10^8. From this we may infer that the internal, cortico-cortical connections of the cortex are at least 10 times, perhaps 100 times more powerful than the connections of the cortex with the external world. It follows that the cortex is a machine that mainly works on its own output or, to put it differently, works in a reflexive mode.

This great internal complexity, compared to the complexity of the input and the output, is characteristic for the cerebral cortex. The fact that the cortex of man (and of other mammals) is the largest piece of gray matter of the whole brain is related to this complexity. Only the cerebellum comes close to the cerebral cortex with its surface area, but not with its volume. The optic tectum, the most impressive "cortex" of lower vertebrates, is far less complex: the number of neurons in the (frog) tectum is about the same as the number of fibers entering the tectum.

There are good reasons to consider the most numerous cell type, the pyramidal cells, as the basic neuronal equipment of the cortex. The great majority of the synapses in the cerebral cortex have pyramidal neurons on both the presynaptic and postsynaptic sides. It is not entirely certain, but it is a fairly safe assumption, that the connections between the pyramidal cells are excitatory. The reasons for this assumption are the following:

1. The cerebral cortex (and especially the hippocampal region) is the piece of nervous tissue most susceptible to epileptic activity (57). If enough neurons are activated, the most diverse stimuli can produce self-sustained seizurelike activity in the cortex. One way of doing this is to make an electric current pass through the tissue. This presumably excites indiscriminately excitatory as well as inhibitory neurons. The fact that a seizure ensues shows that the excitatory connections prevail over the inhibitory ones. It is reasonable, then, to make the pyramidal cells, the most numerous cell type, responsible for the excitatory connections.

2. The fibers of the corpus callosum, which are axons of pyramidal cells, certainly make excitatory connections since they convey epileptic activity from one side of the brain to the other ("mirror focus" (58)). Their excitatory nature has also been directly observed by electrophysiological means (59).

3. The axons of cortical pyramidal cells that reach distant places, such as the spinal cord, make excitatory connections.

A pyramidal cell of average size (in the mouse) has about 5,000 synapses over which it receives excitation. This is shown by measurements of the length of dendrites, by counting the number of so-called dendritic spines per length of dendrite, and from the electron-microscopic observation that most "spines" receive only one synapse. The number of synapses that the axon of a pyramidal cell with all its branches makes is about equal to this number. The question arises as to divergence and convergence in this system of synaptic connections between pyramidal cells. The question can be formulated thus: from how many different neurons do the 5,000 afferent synapses of a pyramidal cell derive, and to how many different cells does one cell distribute its 5,000 efferent connections? The answer: from about 5,000 and to about 5,000 results from geometrical considerations, particularly from the straightness and the sparse branching of the axon collaterals, which only allow multiple connections with the dendritic tree of another pyramidal cell in the rare case that a collateral happens to run parallel to a dendrite (60).

The overall picture is one of a large cortical mixing machine that transmits signals from every cell to as many as possible other cells and inversely allows signals from many other cells to converge on each cell.

The connections between pyramidal cells are collected in two distinct systems of fibers (figure 39). The fibers of the *A-system* are the axons of pyramidal cells, which traverse the white substance and enter the cortex again in different places in order to terminate (mainly) in the upper layers of the cortex. There they make synaptic connections with the so-called apical dendrites of other pyramidal cells. The *B-system* consists of branches of the pyramidal cell axon, which stay within the cortex and make synaptic contact with the so-called basal dendrites of neighboring pyramidal cells.

The assumption that both the A- and the B-terminals of the excitatory pyramidal cell axon have pyramidal cells among their target neurons has not been proved directly by electron-microscopical observation, but it is inescapable on quantitative grounds. The bulk of the postsynaptic sites are furnished by dendritic spines of pyramidal cells. The greater part of the axonal presynaptic specializations again belong to pyramidal cells. The majority of the affer-

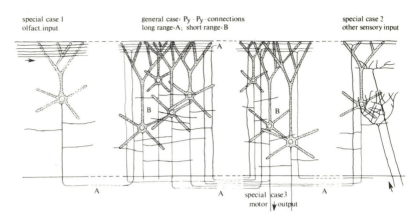

Figure 39

The skeleton cortex: pyramidal cells with long-range (A) and short-range (B) connections. The olfactory input to the upper layers and other sensory input to the middle layers are also shown (from Braitenberg, 1978).

ents of a pyramidal cell must come from pyramidal cells, and vice versa.

The main hypothesis about the role of the pyramidal cells is supported by indirect evidence: if among the afferent fibers of a neuron there are some that often become active simultaneously, the synapses of these fibers are strengthened. I have already mentioned, in the discussion of memory, the observation supporting this assumption. The projection of corresponding points of the right and left visual fields on the visual cortex depends on a learning process in which a fiber from each eye is evidently connected to one and the same cortical neuron—presumably a pyramidal cell—in virtue of their similar activity patterns (figure 31) (6). Rauschecker and Singer (62) showed that this happens according to a rule quite similar to the one postulated by Hebb.

I assume that each pyramidal cell is capable of discovering correlated activity among its afferent fibers all over its dendritic tree. The constellation of afferents whose synapses are strengthened by the learning process consists in general of afferents on the apical dendrites as well as afferents on basal dendrites. Due to the connection of the apical dendrites to distant neurons (A-System) and that of the basal dendrites to neighboring neurons (B-System), in each elementary learning process in one pyramidal cell the information concerning the condition of the whole cortex is brought into relation with information within the context of the area.

This can be further interpreted: the things of our experience, the "terms" of the cortical representation are composed from different sense qualities and are consequently detected by the apical dendritic trees of pyramidal cells as constellations of activity in their long-range cortico-cortical afferents. On the contrary, the rules of the evolution and modification of these terms are more likely specified in terms of individual sensory modalities and are therefore contained within the confines of cortical areas. It would then be the business of basal dendrites to detect these rules in the activity of afferents they receive from neighboring cells of the same area. The distinction of two parts of the dendritic tree, typical of the cortical pyramidal cells, according to this view reflects the logical distinction between *terms* and *relations* between terms. The unitary learning process, which we assume to involve the whole of the dendritic tree, implies that the learning of terms and the learning of their relations condition each other. This is the origin of the idea that made Vehicle II smarter than its predecessors.

If we assign to the pyramidal cells the task of learning sets of afferents with correlated activity, we may even derive from this a role for the inhibitory "stellate cells," which seem to be preferentially located in the places where the external input to the cortex meets the pyramidal cells—in the fourth layer of the cortex and particularly in the primary sensory regions. Let us assume that a pyramidal cell can only learn to recognize (and therefore to strengthen its synapses with) sets of afferents that tend to become active together. It cannot learn to recognize a constellation of activity characterized by some fibers becoming active, and some fibers at the same time remaining inactive. In fact, in order to learn a conjunction of such negated and non-negated terms, the learning mechanism inside the neuron would have to be considerably more complicated than if it only had to recognize conjunctions of positive terms. Still, most of the concepts we learn consist of negated and non-negated qualities: man is a featherless biped, a ring is a disc of a particular material with absence of that material from a central region, and so on.

This difficulty is best dealt with by imagining that each input fiber, besides reaching some cortical pyramidal cells directly through excitatory synapses, inhibits others via interposed inhibitory interneurons. This makes available to the cortical learning mechanism a set of pyramidal cells standing for the corresponding input being active, and another set signaling the corresponding input being inactive. The learning process may limit itself to the detection of simultaneous activity of members of these two sets and thus conjoin negated and non-negated terms with the same ease with which it conjoins non-negated terms.

I recently proposed a model for orientation and direction-sensitive line detectors in the visual cortex, which assigns to a set of inhibitory neurons in area 17 this role of switching the sign of the input (63). This may be just a special case of a general principle of the cortex.

Cell assemblies; embodiments of ideas (Vehicles 7, 10)

Vehicles 10 to 14 operate with ideas that stand for things or situations in their environment, and the ideas are represented in the brains of the vehicles by groups of active elements that are somehow tied together by reciprocal activating connections. We may ask: why are things not represented by single elements or, quite abstractly, by patterns of activity which are not constrained by the condition that the active elements excite each other? The answer is of course: because the vehicles are caricatures of real brains and at present it is again fashionable to think of groups of connected neurons, so-called *cell assemblies* (64), as the carriers of individual items of meaning or, if we wish, as the morphemes in the language of the brain.

It is important to realize that there is no logical reason for this interpretation. Suppose the point is internal representation of things in such a way that any large enough subset of the details that characterize a thing will be sufficient to evoke the thing in its entirety. This is undoubtedly a good principle, since it makes for economical use of channel capacity under the assumption that the existence of things is the main redundancy in the world, with "things" standing for bundles of details each of which, when it presents itself, raises the probability for the rest of them to present themselves as well.* Under these circumstances a Hebbian assembly of all the neurons which individually represent the details of a thing is indeed a good codeword for that thing, since it represents in its internal excitatory connections the conditional probabilities that characterize the thing itself. But a single neuron that receives excitatory synapses from a set of afferents representing the details of a thing is also a good codeword, very much for the same reasons, if its threshold is set appropriately somewhere between the value for "all afferents active" and that for "one afferent active." It, too, will

---

*If you want to grasp the meaning of terms such as channel capacity, redundancy, and conditional probability, you must read more information theory than I can pack into a footnote. There are many introductory texts, one of the best still being Shannon and Weaver's *Mathematical Theory of Communication* (1949).

respond to subsets of the details that characterize the thing, the size of the subset being determined by the threshold.

The reasons why we think again in terms of cell assemblies are more empirical. Cell assemblies have recently gained support from neurophysiology in two ways. First, many years of recording responses of single neurons to sensory stimuli have shown that no very complicated or very unique input is needed to activate a neuron. The most efficient stimuli for cortical neurons are rather elementary configurations of the sensory input, such as moving lines in narrow regions of the visual field (65) or changing frequencies in certain delimited regions of the acoustic spectrum (66). These simple "features" cannot independently carry meaning but must be related to meaningful events in the same way as the phonemes of linguistics are related to words or sentences. The whole meaningful event must be signaled in the brain by a set of neurons, each contributing a particular aspect which that event may have in common with many other events.

The second line of evidence is derived from the neurophysiology of learning. It was one of Hebb's points that cell assemblies representing things in the brain are held together by excitatory connections between the neurons of which they are composed and that these connections are established through a learning process. The most natural way in which such learning could take place is the transformation of a statistical correlation, say, a frequent coincidence of a certain set of elementary features in the input, into synaptic connections between the corresponding neurons. We have already seen how some recent observations on the plasticity of the connections of single neurons can indeed be explained by invoking such a mechanism (67).

The anatomy of the cortex, as I have just sketched it, also makes good sense in terms of the theory of cell assemblies (68). If we want to be ready to build up plenty of cell assemblies, we need plenty of neurons. The cerebral cortex in fact contains about as many neurons as the rest of the brain. These ought to be richly connected, with a high divergence of signals from each neuron to as many as possible other neurons in the cortex. We have already seen that the pyramidal cells do their best in this respect. This divergence (and corresponding convergence) is necessary in order to provide as much freedom as possible for the choice of partners in the development of cell assemblies. Finally, most synapses ought to be excitatory, since cell assemblies are held together by excitatory synapses. About three out of four synapses in the cortex are of type I, presumably excitatory (69).

Threshold control and the pump of thoughts (Vehicles 12, 13, 14)

Threshold control is what makes Vehicle 12 special. There is only indirect evidence for this in animal brains, but it is difficult to see how they could work otherwise, especially mammalian brains with their enormous collection of cortical neurons reciprocally connected by positive feedback, an explosive situation indeed. Threshold control may be more than a necessary evil; in fact, it does introduce interesting dynamics in an otherwise all-too-rigid mechanism of "cell assemblies" and associations. I have shown that something akin to thinking may result from the dynamics of threshold control (70), and Palm (71) has gone a long way toward showing the potentialities of this principle. That this may be chaotic (72), and therefore unpredictable, you may or may not accept as sufficient explanation of the freedom of thought.

On the input side of the threshold control we need a mechanism that can quickly discover the explosive ignition of cell assemblies. A cell assembly may be composed of neurons distributed over wide regions of the cerebral cortex; therefore, this mechanism should receive input from the entire cortex. The piece of gray substance accompanying the cortex of the hemisphere throughout its extent is the caudate nucleus, and it has been shown to receive input from everywhere in an orderly topographical projection (73).

A recent study by Wilson, Hull, and Buchwald (74) provides evidence for very effective propagation of input from different parts of the cerebral cortex throughout the caudate nucleus, quite in accordance with the idea of the caudate nucleus as the detector of overall cortical activity. I suggest that the striatum-caudate complex is part of the mechanism for cortical threshold control probably via the paleostriatum-thalamus loop.

The last two vehicles, introducing the idea of prediction, repeat what has often been discussed by psychologists. I am unable to say whether the idea of optimistic prediction is original with me (75); I presume it has occurred to others. It seems to me sufficient to take away any aura of mystery from goal-directed behavior.

References

1. Cajal, S. R. y. 1898. Structure of the optic chiasm and general theory of the crossing visual pathways. (Estructura del kiasma optico y teoria general de los entrecruzamientos de las vias nervosas.) *Rev. trimest.* micrograf.LLL, quoted in Cajal, 1911.

2. Gaze, R. M. 1958. The representation of the retina on the optic lobe of the frog. *Quart. J. Exp. Physiol.* 43: 209–214.

3. Braitenberg, V. 1967. Patterns of projection in the visual system of the fly. I. Retina-Lamina projections. *Exp. Brain Res.* 3: 271–298.

4. Autrum, H. J., and I. Wiedmann. 1962. Experiments on the optics of the insect eye (appositional eye). (Versuche über den Strahlengang im Insektenauge (Appositonsauge).) *Z. Naturforsch.* 17: 480–482.
   Kirschfeld, K. 1967. The projection of the visual environment on the array of rhabdomeres in the compound eye of Musca. (Die Projektion der optischen Umwelt auf das Raster der Rhabdomere im Komplexauge von Musca.) *Exp. Brain Res.* 3: 248–270.

5. Vigier, P. 1907. The mechanism of the synthesis of the visual perception in compound eye of dipterans. (Mecanisme de la Synthese des impressions lulumineuses recueillies par les yeux composes des dipteres.) *C.R. Acad. Sci. Paris* 122–124.

6. Horridge, G. A., and I. A. Meinertzhagen. 1970. The accuracy of the patterns of connexions of the first- and second-order neurons of the visual system of Calliphora. *Proc. Roy. Soc. B.* 175: 69–82.

7. Braitenberg, V. 1965. Taxis, kinesis and decussation. *Progress in Brain Res.* 17: 210–222.

   Braitenberg, V. 1968. On Chiasms. In: *Neural networks,* edited by E. R. Caianiello. Berlin, Heidelberg, New York: Springer-Verlag, pp. 34–42.

8. Fraenkel, G. S., and D. L. Gunn. 1961. *The orientation of animals. Kineses, taxes and compass reactions.* New York: Dover Publications Inc.

9. Loeb, J. 1890. Heliotropism in animals and its analogy with plant heliotropism. (Der Heliotropismus der Tiere und seine Übereinstimmung mit dem Heliotropismus der Planzen.) Würzburg. p. 118. Quoted in Fraenkel and Gunn, 1961.

10. Roessler, O. E. 1981. An artificial cognitive-plus-motivational system. *Progr. Theor. Biol.* 6: 147–160.

    Koshland, D. E. 1980. *Bacterial chemotaxis as model behavioral system.* New York: Raven Press.

11. Fermi, G., and W. Reichardt. 1963. Optomotor reactions in the fly, Musca domestica. Dependence of the reaction on the space frequency, the velocity and the luminance of moving periodic patterns. (Optomotorische Reaktion der Fliege Musca domestica. Abhängigkeit von der Reaktion der Wellenlänge, der Geschwindigkeit, dem Kontrast und der mitleren Leuchtdichte bewegter periodischer Muster.) *Kybernetik* 2: 15–28.

12. Reichardt, W. 1970. The insect eye as a model for analysis of uptake, transduction and processing of optical data in the nervous system. 34. Physikertagung 1969, Salzburg, Plenarvorträge. Stuttgart: B. G. Teubner.

13. Fraenkel, G. S., and D. L. Gunn. 1961. *The orientation of animals. Kineses, taxes and compass reactions.* New York: Dover Publications Inc.

    Mast, S. O. 1923. Photic orientation in insects, with special reference to the dronefly, Eristalis tenax, and the robber-fly, Erax rufibarbis. *J. Exp. Zol.* 38: 109–205.

14. Ewert, J. P. 1980. *Neuroethology. An introduction to the neurophysiological fundamentals of behaviour.* Berlin, Heidelberg, New York: Springer-Verlag.

15. McCulloch, W. S., and W. H. Pitts. 1943. A logical calculus of ideas immanent in nervous activity. *Bull. Math. Biophys.* 5: 115–133.

16. Creed, R. S., D. Denny-Brown, J. Eccles, E. G. T. Liddell, and C. S. Sherrington. 1932. *Reflex activity of the spinal cord.* Oxford: Clarendon Press.

17. Eccles, J. C. 1964. *The physiology of synapses.* Berlin, Göttingen, Heidelberg, New York: Springer-Verlag.

18. Kleene, S. C. 1956. Representation of events in nerve nets and finite automata.

In: *Automata studies,* edited by C. E. Shannon and J. McCarthy. Princeton, New Jersey: Princeton University Press.

Arbib, M. A. 1964. *Brains, machines and mathematics.* New York: McGraw Hill.

19. Von Neumann, J. 1956. Probabilistic logics and the synthesis of reliable organisms from unreliable components. In: *Automata studies,* edited by C. E. Shannon and J. McCarthy. Princeton, New Jersey: Princeton University Press.

20. Turing, A. M. On computable numbers, with an application to the Entscheidungsproblem. *Proc. London Math. Society.* Ser. 2, 42: 230–265 (1936) and 42: 534–546 (1937).

Minsky, M. L. 1967. *Computation: finite and infinite machines.* Englewood Cliffs, New Jersey: Prentice-Hall.

Sampson, J. R. 1976. *Adaptive information processing. An introductory survey.* New York, Heidelberg, Berlin: Springer-Verlag.

21. Dawkins, R. 1976. *The selfish gene.* Oxford: Oxford University Press.

22. Darwin, Ch. 1859. *The origin of species.* New American Library. Mentor paperback, 1958.

Fisher, R. A. 1958. *The genetical theory of natural selection.* New York: Dover.

Mayr, E. 1970. *Population, species, and evolution.* Cambridge, Mass.: Harvard University Press.

23. Uttley, A. M. 1956. Conditional probability machines and conditioned reflexes. In: *Automata studies,* edited by C. E. Shannon and J. McCarthy. Princeton, New Jersey: Princeton University Press.

24. Steinbuch, K. 1969. The learning matrix. (Die Lernmatrix.) *Kybernetik.* 1: 36–45.

25. Hebb, D. O. 1949. *Organization of behavior.* New York: Wiley and Son.

26. Sutton, R. S., and A. G. Barto. 1981. Toward a modern theory of adaptive networks: expectation and prediction. *Psychol. Rev.* 88: 135.

27. Hubel, D. H., and T. N. Wiesel. 1965. Binocular interaction in striate cortex of kittens reared with artificial squint. *J. Neurophysiol.* 28: 1041–1059.

Wiesel, T. N., and D. H. Hubel. 1965. Comparison of the effects of unilateral and bilateral eye closure on cortical unit responses in kitten. *J. Neurophysiol.* 28: 1029–1040.

28. Baer, A. 1905. Contemporaneous electrical stimulation of two regions of the cerebral cortex of an unrestrained dog. (Über gleichzeitige elektrische Reizung zweier Großhirnstellen am ungehemmten Hunde.) *Pflüger's Arch. Ges. Physiol.* 106: 523–567.

Loucks, R. B. 1933. Preliminary report of a technique for stimulation or destruction of tissues beneath the integument and the establishing of conditioned reactions with faradization of the cerebral cortex. *J. Comp. Psychol.* 16: 439–444.

29. Bennett, E. L., M. C. Diamond, D. Krech, and M. R. Rosenzweig. 1964. Chemical and anatomical plasticity of brain. *Science* 146: 610–619.

Diamond, M. C., D. Krech, and M. R. Rosenzweig. 1964. The effects of an enriched environment on the histology of the rat cerebral cortex. *J. Comp. Neur.* 123: 111–120.

Walsh, R. N., O. E. Budtz-Olsen, L. E. Penny, and R. A. Cummins. 1969. The effects of environmental complexity on the histology of the rat hippocampus. *J. Comp. Neur.* 137: 361–366.

Szeligo, F., and C. P. Leblond. 1977. Response of the three main types of glial cells of cortex and corpus callosum in rats handled during suckling exposed to enriched, control and impoverished environments following weaning. *J. Comp. Neur.* 172: 247–264.

30. Schüz, A. 1978. Some facts and hypotheses concerning dendritic spines and learning. In: *Architectonics of the cerebral cortex,* edited by M. A. B. Brazier and H. Petsche. New York: Raven Press, pp. 129–135.

Schüz, A. 1981. Prenatal maturation and postnatal changes in the guinea pig cortex: a histological study of a natural deprivation experiment. I. Prenatal development. (Pränatale Reifung und postnatale Veränderungen im Cortex des Meerschweinchens: Mikroskopische Auswertung eines natürlichen Deprivationsexperimentes. I. Pränatale Entwicklung.) *J. Hirnforsch.* 22: 93–111.

31. Schüz, A. 1981. Prenatal maturation and postnatal changes in the guinea pig cortex: a histological study of a natural deprivation experiment. II. Postnatal changes. (Pränatale Reifung und postnatale Veränderungen im Cortex des Meerschweinchens: Auswertung eines natürlichen Deprivationsexperimentes. II. Postnatale Veränderungen.) *J. Hirnforsch.* 22: 113–127.

32. See for instance the impressive collection of visual areas in the papers by Tusa, Palmer and Rosenquist, by Van Essen, Maunsell and Bixby, by Allmann, Baker, Newsome and Petersen and by Gros, Bruce, Desimone, Fleming, and Gattas in the volume *Cortical sensory organization, Vol. 2: multiple visual areas,* edited by Clinton N. Woolsey. Clifton, New Jersey: Humana Press, 1981.

33. Minsky, M. 1975. *Semantic information processing.* Cambridge, Mass.: The MIT Press.

34. Lieblich, I., and M. A. Arbib. 1982. Multiple representations of space underlying behavior. *The Behavioral and Brain Sciences.* 5: 627–659.

35. Barlow, H. B., R. M. Hill, and W. R. Levick. 1964. Retinal ganglion cells responding selectively to directions and speed of image motion in the rabbit. *J. Physiol.* 173: 377–407.

36. Hassenstein, B., and W. Reichardt. 1956. System theoretic analysis of temporal factors, of sequence and sign in the perception of movement by the beetle, Chlorophanus. (Systemtheoretische Analyse der Zeit, Reihenfolgen und Vorzeichenauswertung bei der Bewegungsperzeption des Rüsselkäfers Chlorophanus.) *Z. Naturforsch.* 11b: 513–524.

    Hassenstein, B. 1958. Perception of movement of figural and irregular patterns. (Über die Wahrnehmung der Bewegung von Figuren und unregelmäßigen Helligkeitsmustern.) *Zeitschrift f. vergl. Physiol.* 40: 556–592.

    Reichardt, W., and D. Varju. 1959. Transfer functions in the visual perception of movement. (Übertragungseigenschaften im Auswertesystem für das Bewegungssehen.) *Z.f. Naturforschung.* 14b (10): 674–689.

37. Fermi, G., and W. Reichardt. 1963. Optomotor reactions in the fly Musca domestica. Dependence on wave length, velocity, contrast and average luminance of moving periodic patterns. (Optomotorische Reaktion der Fliege Musca domestica. Abhängigkeit der Reaktion von der Wellenlänge, der Geschwindigkeit, dem Kontrast und der mittleren Leuchtdichte bewegter periodischer Muster.) *Kybernetik* 2: 15–28.

    Reichardt, W., and T. Poggio. 1976. Visual control of orientation behaviour in the fly. Part I. A quantitative analysis. *Quart. Rev. Biophys.* 3: 311–375.

    Poggio, T., and W. Reichardt. 1976. Visual control of orientation behaviour in the fly. Part II. Towards the underlying neural interaction. *Quart. Rev. Biophysics* 9, 3: 377–438.

38. Braitenberg, V. 1973. *On the texture of brains.* New York, Heidelberg, Berlin: Springer-Verlag.

39. Mach, quoted in Ratliff, F. 1965. *Mach bands.* San Francisco: Holden Day.

40. Bekesy, G. v. 1960. *Experiments in hearing.* New York: McGraw Hill.

41. Hartline, H. K., and F. Ratliff. 1957. Inhibitory interaction of receptor units in the eye of Limulus. *J. Gen. Physiol.* 40: 357–367.

42. Reichardt, W. 1961. On the optical resolution in Limulus. (Über das optische Auflösungsvermögen von "Limulus.") *Kybernetik* 1: 59–69.

    Varju, D. 1965. On the theory of lateral inhibition. In: *Cybernetics of neural processes,* edited by E. R. Caianiello. Rome: C.N.R.

43. Szentagothai, J. 1967. In: *Eccles, Ito and Szentagothai: The cerebellum as a neuronal machine.* Berlin, Heidelberg, New York: Springer.

44. Beurle, R. L. 1956. Properties of a mass of cells capable of regenerating pulses. *Proc. R. Soc. Lond. Ser. B.* 240: 55.

   Wilson, H. R., and J. D. Cowan. 1973. A mathematical theory of the functional dynamics of cortical and thalamic nervous tissue. *Kybernetik* 13: 35.

45. Hubel, D. H., and T. N. Wiesel. 1972. Laminar and columnar distribution of geniculo-cortical fibers in the macaque monkey. *J. Comp. Neurol.* 146: 421–450.

46. Köhler, W. 1933. *Psychologische Probleme.* Berlin: Springer.

   Wertheimer, M. 1923. Experimental contributions to the theory of form. (Untersuchungen zur Lehre von der Gestalt.) *Psychol. Forsch.* 4.

   Petermann, B. 1929. Die Wertheimer-Koffka-Köhlersche Gestalttheorie und das Gestaltproblem. Leipzig: Barth.

   For recent developments see:

   Gibson, J. J. 1950. *The perception of the visual world.* Boston: Houghton Mifflin Co.

   Julesz, B. 1971. *Foundation of cyclopean perception.* Chicago and London: The University of Chicago Press.

   Metzger, W. 1975. *Gesetze des Sehens.* Frankfurt: Verlag Waldemar Kramer; and a series of contributions of the Italian school: Kanisza, G., F. Metelli, G. Vicario, and P. Bozzi, in the *Rivista di Psicologia* and the *Giornale Italiano di Psicologia.*

47. Minsky, M., and S. Papert. 1969. *Perceptrons.* Cambridge, Mass.: The MIT Press.

   Braddick, O. J., and A. C. Sleigh. 1983. *Physical and biological processing of images.* Berlin, Heidelberg, New York: Springer.

48. Braitenberg, V. 1983. In search of morphemes in the brain. *Giornale Italiano di Psicologia.* 10: 521–540.

49. At the European Neuroscience Society meeting, Brighton, 1980.

50. Kanisza, G. 1974. Contours without gradients or cognitive contours. *Giornale Italiano di Psicologia* 1.

   Brunswik, E. 1935. Quoted in Metzger 1975. See note 46.

   Kennedy, J. M. 1974. Quoted in Metzger 1975. See note 46.

51. Lieblich, I., and M. Arbib, 1982. See note 34.

52. Barlow, H. B., and B. C. Reeves. 1978. The versatility and absolute efficiency of detecting mirror symmetry in random dot displays. *Vision Res.* Vol. 19: 783–793.

53. Scheffers, G. 1911. *Lehrbuch der Mathematik,* 2nd edition. Leipzig: Veit and Co.

54. Hubel, D. H., and T. N. Wiesel. 1959. Receptive fields of single neurones in the cat's striate cortex. *J. Physiol.* (Lond.) 148: 574–591.

    Hubel, D. H., and T. N. Wiesel. 1977. Functional architecture of macaque monkey visual cortex. Ferrier Lecture. *Proc. R. Soc. Lond. B.* 198: 1–59.

55. Tunturi, A. R. 1962. Frequency arrangement in anterior ectosylvian auditory cortex of dog. *Am. J. Physiol.* 203: 185.

    Evans, E. F. 1968. Upper and lower levels of the auditory system: A contrast of structure and function. In: *Neural networks,* edited by E. R. Caianiello. Berlin, Heidelberg, New York: Springer.

56. Braitenberg, V. 1978. Cortical architectonics: general and areal. In: *Architectonics of the cerebral cortex,* edited by M. A. B. Brazier and H. Petsche. New York: Raven Press, pp. 443–465.

    Braitenberg, V. 1978. Cell assemblies in the cerebral cortex. In: *Lecture notes in biomathematics,* Vol. 21, edited by R. Heim and G. Palm. Berlin, Heidelberg, New York: Springer, pp. 171–188.

57. Jasper, H. H. 1969. Mechanisms of propagation: extracellular studies. In: *Brain mechanisms of the epilepsies,* edited by H. H. Jasper, A. A. Ward, and A. Pope. Boston: Little, Brown and Company.

58. Morell, F. 1961. Lasting changes in synaptic organization produced by continuous neuronal bombardment. In: *CIOMS symposium on brain mechanisms and learning,* edited by A. Fessard. London: Blackwell, pp. 375–392.

59. Renaud, quoted by Gloor, P. 1972. In: *Synchronization of EEG activity in epilepsies,* edited by H. Petsche and M. A. B. Brazier. Wien, New York: Springer.

60. Braitenberg, V. 1978. Cell assemblies. See note 56.

61. Hubel, D. H., and T. N. Wiesel. 1965. Binocular interaction. See note 27.

    Wiesel, T. N., and D. H. Hubel. 1965. Comparison of the effects. See note 27.

62. Rauschecker, J. P., and W. Singer. 1981. The effects of early visual experience on the cat's visual cortex and their possible explanation by Hebb synapses. *J. Physiol.* 310: 215–239.

63. Braitenberg, V. 1983. Explanation of orientation columns in terms of a homogeneous network of neurons in the visual cortex. *Neuroscience Abstracts.* 9: 474.

64. Hebb, D. O. 1949. *The organization of behavior.* New York: John Wiley.

65. Hubel, D. H., and T. N. Wiesel. 1959. Receptive fields of single neurones in the cat's striate cortex. *J. Physiol.* (Lond.) 148: 574–591.

66. Evans, E. F. 1968. Upper and lower levels of the auditory system: A contrast of structure and function. In: *Neural networks,* edited by E. R. Caianiello. Berlin, Heidelberg, New York: Springer.

Aertsen, A. M. H. J., and P. I. M. Johannesma. 1981. The spectrotemporal receptive field. A functional characteristic of auditory neurons. *Biol. Cybern.* 42: 133–143.

67. Hubel, D. H., and T. N. Wiesel. 1965. Binocular interaction. See note 27.

Wiesel, T. N., and D. H. Hubel. 1965. Comparison of the effects. See note 27.

Blakemore, C., and G. F. Cooper. 1971. Modification of the visual cortex by experience. *Brain Res.* 31: 366.

Hirsch, H. V. B., and D. N. Spinelli. 1971. Modification of the distribution of receptive field orientation in cats by selective visual exposure during development. *Exp. Brain Res.* 13: 1–43.

68. Braitenberg, V. 1978. Cell assemblies. See note 56.

69. Wolff, J. R. 1976. Quantitative analysis of topography and development of synapses in the visual cortex. *Exp. Brain Res.* Suppl. 1: 259–263.

Uchizono, K. 1966. Characteristics of excitatory and inhibitory synapses in the central nervous system of the cat. *Nature* 207: 642.

70. Braitenberg, V. 1978. Cell assemblies. See note 56.

Braitenberg, V. 1977. *On the texture of brains. Neuroanatomy for the cybernetically minded.* Berlin, Heidelberg, New York: Springer.

71. Palm, G. 1982. *Neural assemblies. An alternative approach to artificial intelligence.* Berlin, Heidelberg, New York: Springer-Verlag.

72. Myrberg, P. J. 1958. Iteration of real polynomials of the 2nd degree. (Iteration der reellen Polynome 2ten Grades.) *I. Am. Acad. Sc. Fenn.* 251A: 1–10.

73. Webster, K. E. 1965. The cortico-striatal projection in the cat. *J. Anat.* 99: 329–335.

Dray, A. 1980. The physiology and pharmacology of mammalian basal ganglia. *Progr. Neurobiol.* 14: 221–335.

74. Wilson, J. S., C. D. Hull, and N. A. Buchwald. 1983. Intracellular studies of the convergence of sensory input on caudate neurons of cat. *Brain Res.* 270: 197–208.

75. Braitenberg, V. Gehirngespinste. Neuroanatomie für kybernetisch Interessierte. Berlin, Heidelberg, New York: Springer, 1973. Revised English translation: *On the texture of brains. Neuroanatomy for the cybernetically minded.* Berlin, Heidelberg, New York: Springer, 1977.